History of Nations

" From Adam PBUH to 300 B.C "

1

Ibn al-Jawzi (1116 CE -1200 CE)

Alreshah.net

Canada

Copyright © 2018-20 by **Alreshah**

All rights reserved. No part of this publication may be reproduced, distributed, or transmitted in any form or by any means, without prior written permission.

Alreshah
www.Alreshah.net

If any error is found, please contact us through our website alreshah.net.

Book Layout © 2017 BookDesignTemplates.com

History of Natioans 1 / Ibn al-Jawzi. -- 1st ed.
ISBN: 978-1-989875-00-1

Contents

Introduction 4

Tale of Adam (PBUH) 6

Tale of the Caliphate of Seth after his Father Adam (PBUH)...19

Tale of Noah (PBUH) 25

Tale of events during the time between Noah and Abraham.....31

Tale of Abraham (PBUH) 35

Event of Abraham's death (PBUH) 57

Tale of Job (PBUH) 71

Tale of Moses (PBUH) 77

Tale of Joshua ibn Nun (PBUH) 109

Tale of Elias (Elijah) (PBUH) 114

The End 129

• CHAPTER 1 •

Introduction

In the name of God, The Entirely Merciful, the Especially Merciful

This is the translation of the first part in a sequence of books written by Imam Abd al-Raḥmān b. ʿAlī b. Muḥammad Abu 'l-Farash b. al-Jawzi, known as Ibn al-Jawzī. He was an Arab Muslim jurisconsult, preacher, orator, heresiographer, traditionist, historian, judge, hagiographer, and philologist who lived in Baghdad during the twelfth century.

In this book, he collected what was known in his time about the nation's history. As the reader will note, this book focused first on parts more toward the Middle East region and on the prophets known to Jews and Christians. The reason behind this is that Baghdad was the heart of the Islamic world, and most of the other nations' knowledge had been concentrated in Baghdad in the Golden Age of the Islamic Empire.

History of Natioans (1)

It is essential to understand that the first and second part of this book, until 600 AD, was based on what the Imam read and gathered from Israelites known to him in his time. So, similarities might be found between the historical events mentioned in those two parts and Biblical stories.

Starting from the end of the second part onward, the authentication differs hugely, as those are more related to Islamic history and the states surrounding the Islamic empire. The spread of knowledge and literacy within the Islamic world resulted in better record-keeping, and references to an event were recorded in different documents.

That what makes this book one of the important books in the history of the region, especially from 600 AD to the author's death, which will be in part three onward.

• CHAPTER 2 •

Tale of Adam (PBUH)

It was narrated that Abu Musa quoted that the Prophet (PBUH) saying: "God created Adam from a handful which he took from the whole of the earth ; so the descendants of Adam are formed in accordance with the earth: some are red, some are white, some are black, some are a mixture, also smooth and rough, bad and good".

As for the day on which Adam was created, it was narrated that Abu Lubabah ibn Abdul Mundhir said: "The Prophet (PBUH) said: 'Friday is the chief of days, the greatest day for God. It is greater for God than the Day of Adha (Greater Bairum; the Feast of Sacrifice) and the Day of Fitr (the Lesser Bairum; the feast of breaking Ramadan fasting). It has five characteristics: On it God created Adam; on it God sent down Adam to the earth; on it there is a time during which God gives the slave what he asks, so long as he does not ask for anything forbidden; on it the Doomsday will be. There is no angel who is close to God, no heaven, no earth, no wind, no mountain, and no sea that does not ask God for forgiveness on (in another narration, fear) Friday.'"

Chapter

Assuddi reported: When God, Might and Sublime, created Adam, He said to angels: When I have breathed into him from My soul, then fall down to him in prostration. The soul entered Adam through his head, then he sneezed. So angels said to him: Say Alhamdulillah (Praise be to God). He said so and God replied: "O Adam, may your Lord have mercy upon you". When the soul entered his eyes, he saw fruits of the Heaven. And when the soul entered his mouth, he craved for food, so he bound quickly before the soul reached his legs. For that, God says: "Man was created of haste". "خُلِقَ الإِنسَانُ مِنْ عَجَلٍ" (21:37). Then, all of angels prostrated to Adam except Satan.

It was narrated that Anas ibn Malik reported that the Prophet (PBUH) saying: "When God fashioned Adam in the Heaven, He left him as He liked him to leave. Then Satan roamed round him to see what actually that was and when he found him hollow from within, he recognized that he had been created with a disposition that he would not have control over himself".

Abu Huraira reported that the Prophet (PBUH) said: "God created Adam (PBUH), and his length was 60 cubits. God told him: 'Go and greet those (a group of angels who were sitting down) and listen to how they answer you. It is your greeting and the greeting of your descendants.' He said: 'Peace be upon you,' and they replied, 'Peace be upon you and the mercy of God.' They added, 'and the mercy of God. All the ones who enter the Heaven will have Adam's form and length, then mankind kept getting shorter until now (i.e. each generation grew shorter than the generation before, and that decrease in height ended with this nation".

Tale of Events Happening during the Era of Adam

These events are divided into three sections: The first one includes what happened to Adam in the heaven. The second one is about what happened to Adam when he was in the Heaven (i.e. Paradise). The third one includes what happened to Adam in the earth.

Tale of the First Section

[What happened to Adam in the heaven]

When God finished creating Adam and breathed the soul into him, He taught him all of names. Al Hasan said: God taught Adam the names of things like: These are horses, those are mules and camels, the jinn, and wild beasts. And Rubai' ibn Anas said: God taught Adam the names of angels. The truth is that God taught him the names of whole things. The greatest event happened in the heaven during the era of Adam was the refusal of Satan to prostrate to him out of arrogance.

Tale of the Second Section

[What happened to Adam in the Paradise]

After angels prostrated to Adam and Satan was expelled, Adam dwelled in the Paradise where he was allowed to eat fruits from all trees except only one. Assuddi narrated: When Adam dwelled it, he was alone. He fell asleep and when he got up he found a woman. He asked her: Who are you and why were you created? She replied: I am a woman created for you to dwell in security with me. Angels asked Adam to test his knowledge: What is her name? He replied: Eve. They asked him: Why was she named so? He said: Because she was created from a living thing. Then, God said: O' Adam, dwell with your wife in the Heaven.

Another event happened also in the Heaven was that Satan tempted Adam to eat fruit from the forbidden tree. He said: "O' Adam, shall I direct you to the tree of eternity". "يَا آدَمُ هَلْ أَدُلُّكَ عَلَى شَجَرَةِ الْخُلْدِ" (20:120).

Accordingly, it was happened that Adam was expelled from the Heaven. Scholars said: When Adam and Eve committed the sin of eating fruit from the forbidden tree, God made them get out of the Heaven and descended them and their enemy Satan to the earth. God says: "Go down, [all of you], as enemies to one another". " اهْبِطُوا بَعْضُكُمْ لِبَعْضٍ عَدُوٌّ" (2:36).

Tale of the Period of Adam's dwelling in the Heaven

It was said by Al Hasan Al Basri that Adam stayed in the Heaven for forty three years and four months (according to the time of the earth).

Tale of the Time when Adam got out of the Heaven

Saad ibn Ebada narrated that the Prophet (PBUH) said: "Adam was created on Friday and sent down from the Heaven to the earth on Friday".

Tale of the place to which Adam descended

Ali ibn Abu Talib, ibn Abbas, Qatada and Abu Al 'Alia said: Adam descended from the Heaven to India. On the other hand, it was said by others: He descended on Serandib, Eve descended on Jeddah in Mecca and Satan descended on Maysan. It was also said that the mountain on which Adam descended was the nearest one to the heaven. But there is no evidence in the Holy Qur'an nor in the Sunnah in respect of the place on which Adam, Eve, Satan descended.

Tale of the Third Section

What happened to Adam in the earth

On the earth, Adam kept crying until God forgave him. He received from God some words which he said. Then, his repentance became approved. This is clear in God's saying:

"Then Adam received from his Lord [some] words, and He accepted his repentance. Indeed, it is He who is the Accepting of repentance, the Merciful". " فَتَلَقَّىٰ آدَمُ مِن رَّبِّهِ كَلِمَاتٍ فَتَابَ عَلَيْهِ إِنَّهُ هُوَ التَّوَّابُ الرَّحِيمُ" (2:37). There are different interpretations by scholars regarding what these words are. For instance, Mujahid said about God's saying: "Then Adam received from his Lord [some] words". " فَتَلَقَّىٰ آدَمُ مِن رَّبِّهِ كَلِمَاتٍ" (2:37), these words are referred to in God's saying: "Our Lord, we have wronged ourselves, and if You do not forgive us and have mercy upon us, we will surely be among the losers". " رَبَّنَا ظَلَمْنَا أَنفُسَنَا وَإِن لَّمْ تَغْفِرْ لَنَا وَتَرْحَمْنَا لَنَكُونَنَّ مِنَ الْخَاسِرِينَ" (7:23).

Among the events happened on the earth is that God, Might and Sublime, sent down to the earth one of the corundum of the Heaven. He put it in the place of the Kaaba. Then, He commanded Adam to go to Mecca in order to perform Tawaf (walk) around the Kaaba.

Other event is that God brought forth from Adam his offspring. And he talked to them saying: "Am I not your Lord?" They said, "Yes, we have testified." [This] - lest you should say on the day of Resurrection, "Indeed, we were of this unaware" "ألست بربكم قالوا بلى شهدنا أن تقولوا يوم القيامة إنا كنا عن هذا غافلين" (7:172).

With Regard to Events

Ubayy ibn Kaab interpreted God's saying "And [mention] when your Lord took from the children of Adam - from their

"وإذ أخذ ربك من بني آدم من ظهورهم ذريتهم" loins - their descendants" (7:172), as he said: God gathered the children of Adam and He made them mates, then He formed them and made them speak, then He took from them a covenant. God says: "and made them testify of themselves, [saying to them], 'Am I not your Lord?'" "وأشهدهم على أنفسهم ألست بربكم" (7:172), ibn Kaab interpreted this saying: God said I make the seven heavens, the seven earths and your father Adam testify of you lest you say on the Doomsday we were unaware of this. Know that there is no Lord but only me and do not associate anything with me. I will send down to you My Holy Books and messengers in order to remind you of My covenant. They said: We testify that You are our Lord, there is no Lord other than You. Then, God made Adam look attentively at them. So, he saw among them one that is rich, another is poor, one is good formed, other one is not. So, he asked God about the reason for not making all of them like each other, God replied him: I like to be praised. Then Adam saw the prophets appearing with light as if there were lamps among them. They were pertained to another covenant with regard to God's message and prophecy. This is referred to in God's saying: "And [mention, O Muhammad], when We took from the prophets their covenant and from you and from Noah and Abraham and Moses and Jesus, the son of Mary; and We took

وإذ أخذنا من النبيين ميثاقهم ومنك ومن نوح " ."from them a solemn covenant
(33:7). "وإبراهيم وموسى وعيسى ابن مريم وأخذنا منهم ميثاقًا غليظًا"

It was narrated by Omar ibn Al Khattab said: "When the Prophet (PBUH) was questioned about the verse "And [mention] when your Lord took from the children of Adam - from their loins - their descendants and made them testify of themselves, [saying to them], "Am I not your Lord?" They said, "Yes, we have testified." [This] - lest you should say on the day of Resurrection, "Indeed, we were of this unaware" "" وإذ أخذ ربك من بني آدم من ظهورهم ذريتهم وأشهدهم على أنفسهم ألست بربكم قالوا بلى شهدنا أن تقولوا يوم القيامة إنا كنا عن هذا غافلين (7:172), He heard the Prophet saying about it: "God created Adam and brought forth – from his loin – his offspring, saying: I have these for the Heaven and these will do the deeds of those who go to the Heaven. He then brought forth from his loin another offspring, saying: I have created these for the Hell, and they will do the deeds of those who go to the Hell. A man asked: What is the good of doing anything, Messenger of God? The Messenger of God (PBUH) said: When God creates a servant for the Heaven, He employs him in doing the deeds of those who will go to the Heaven, so that his final action before death is one of the deeds of those who go to the Heaven, for which He will bring him into the Heaven. But when He creates a servant for the Hell, He employs him in doing the deeds of those who will go to the Hell, so that his final action before death is one of the deeds of those who go to the Hell, for which He will bring him into the Hell".

It was narrated by Abu Huraira and others that the Prophet (PBUH) said: "After God created Adam, He said to him – while His Two Hands were closed – 'Choose which of them you wish.' He said: 'I chose the right, my Lord, and both of the Hands of my Lord are right and blessed.' Then He extended it, and there was Adam and his offspring in it.' So he said: 'O' my Lord, who are these?' God said: 'These are your offspring'. Each one of them had his age written between his eyes. In addition, each one of them had a ray of light between his eyes. But among them there was a man who was the most illuminating of them – or among the most illuminated of them. He said: 'O Lord! Who is this?' He said: 'This is a man from the latter nations of your offspring, your son Dawud (David), I wrote his lifespan to be forty years.' He said: 'O Lord! Add to his age.' He said: 'That is what I have written for him.' He said: 'O' Lord! Give him sixty of my years.' He said: 'So you shall have it.'" He said: "Then, he resided in the Heaven as long as God willed, then he was cast from it, so Adam was counting for himself." He said: "So the Angel of death came to him, and Adam said to him: 'You are hasty, one thousand years were written for me.' He said: 'Of course! But you gave sixty years to your son David.' So, he rejected, and his offspring rejected, and he forgot, and his offspring forgot." He said: "So ever since that day, what is written and witnessed has been decreed."

With Regard to Events, the Birth of Children of Adam

Among the events which happened to Adam was that Eve gave birth to forty children, males and females, by being pregnant for twenty times; as she gave birth to twins – a male and a female – in each time of pregnancy. The first twins were Cain and his twin sister Qaleema. And the last twins were Abd Al Mogheeth and his twin sister Amat Al Mogheeth.

Of this offspring, a male could marry anyone of his sisters as he desired except his twin sister. She was not lawful to him.

Abu Jaafar Al Tabari said: There was a gap of five years after Abel's being killed, then Seth was born. On the birthday of Seth, Adam was one hundred and thirty years old, as narrated by Abu Saleh from ibn Abbas.

With Regard to Events, Prophecy of Adam

In addition to the previous events, God, Might and Sublime, made Adam a prophet and a messenger to his offspring. And He sent down to him twenty one sheets of paper which he was taught by Gabriel. Abu Dharr narrated: I asked Prophet Muhammad (PBUH): Who is the first prophet? He replied: "Adam". I said: Was he a prophet? He replied: "Yes, he was". In respect to this, he was admonishing his offspring.

With Regard to Events, Cain Murdered his Brother Abel

It was happened also that Cain killed his brother Abel. Concerning the reason for killing Abel, Assuddi mentioned that Adam used to marry the male from each pregnancy to the female of another pregnancy, and that the sister of Cain was more beautiful than the sister of Abel. Cain wanted to keep his sister and marry her himself, but Adam did not let him, so when he insisted, he instructed them both to make an offering (sacrifice to God). Cain offered a sheaf of corn, because he was a grower of crops, and Abel offered a fat lamb, because he kept livestock. Fire came down (from heaven) and consumed the offering of Abel, but not that of Cain [i.e., Abel's offering was accepted and Cain's was not], and that was the cause of the trouble between them.

After Cain had killed Abel, he did not know how to bury him until God sent two crows fighting one another till one of them killed the other then dig a hole in which it put the killed crow. Thereat, Cain said as mentioned in the Holy Qur'an "Have I failed to be like this crow?" "أعجزت أن أكون مثل هذا الغراب" (5:31).

Abdullah (ibn Mas'ud) reported that the Prophet (PBUH) said: "No person is killed unjustly but the first son of Adam (i.e. Cain) will have a part of the burden of the crime, because he was the first one to introduce the precedence of killing".

With Regard to Events

History of Natioans (1)

After Cain had killed his brother, he went to Yemen. His offspring became massive and they began to fight sons of Adam. So Adam willed descendants of Seth not to marry descendants of Cain. The earlier made Adam away from the latter and protect him. Adam was asking God's forgiveness for descendants of Seth only.

With Regard to Events,

Death of Adam (PBUH)

God, the Almighty, made Adam live for one thousand years. Muhammad ibn Isaac said: When Adam came to die, he called his son, Seth, and taught him the hours of night and day, and how to worship God, the Truth, in every hour throughout the day. Adam wrote his will to Seth.

Abu Jaafar Al Tabari said: Adam remained sick for eleven days before dying. He brought his will to his son Seth and commanded him to hide it from Cain. So, Seth and his offspring hid what they had of knowledge. Then, Cain and his offspring had no beneficial knowledge. Adam died on Friday.

There are many sayings about the place where Adam (PBUH) was buried. But there is no definite proof of the place of Adam's grave.

CHAPTER 3

Tale of the Caliphate of Seth after his Father Adam (PBUH)

Seth, the son of Adam, was the executor of the will of his father.

Tale of Events that happened during the Statehood of Seth

It was happened that the mother of Seth, Eve, died. There was a gap of only one year after the death of Adam then she died.

With Regard to the Events that began during the Era of Adam and lasted after his Death

When Cain murdered his brother, he escaped to Yemen. Then, Satan came to him and said: The offering of your brother had been accepted because he was worshipping fire. So, set fire for you and your descendents as well and worship it. He did so and was the first one to worship fire.

The offspring of Cain were tyrants and oppressors. Then his offspring ceased to exist and so did Adam's sons, except the offspring of Seth.

Concerning Seth

Enos was a son born to Seth during the life of his father Adam. Seth passed his will to Enos in respect of undertaking the policy of monarchy and directing the affairs of nationals in the same manner of his father. Enos was the first one to plant palms and grains and was given wisdom. He lived for nine hundred and five years.

After that, Enos had a son called Kenan during the life of Adam also. Consequently, Enos passed his will to Kenan. Kenan passed it to his son Mahalalel who was following his father's manner. Mahalalel was also born during the life of Adam. Then, Mahalalel passed his will to his son Yard. It was said that Yard was also born during the life of Adam. Then Akhanukh, also known as Enoch – Prophet Idris (PBUH) – was born to Jared. Narrators hardly agree with each other about these names.

Chapter

Jared, the father of Idris, lived for nine hundred years. Abu Saleh narrated from ibn Abbas: Idols were worshipped during the era of Jared.

History of Natioans (1)

It was said that Wadd, Suwa', Yaghuth, Ya'uq and Nasr were righteous people. After their death, their relatives and natives became so sad for their loss. So, a man of the descendants of Cain said to them: O people, shall I make for you five idols with the same form as those five righteous people? They agreed. And he did so. But the truth is that these five idols were made after the coming of Noah. The nation of Noah may have made the idols following the deed of their precedents.

Tale of Idris (PBUH)

His name is Enoch ibn Jared ibn Mahalalel ibn Kenan ibn Enos ibn Seth ibn Adam. He is called Idris in Arabic because of his devotion to the study of the sacred books of his ancestors Adam and Seth; he is the first one studying the written revelation. Ibn Abbas said: "The first prophet comes after Adam is Idris, (PBUH); He is Enoch ibn Jared. God says to him: 'I would raise for you every day the same amount of the deeds of all Adam's children in a year'– perhaps meaning of his time only. Satan envies him and his people did not obey, but God raised him to a high station and entered him the Heaven.

Scholars of biographies said: God made Idris a prophet during the lifetime of Adam, when the latter was 622 years and revealed thirty portions of revealed scripture. He invited, preached and commanded his people to obey God not the devil.

He is the first person to write with a pen, cut and saw clothes. He was raised while he was 365 years old and his father was still alive.

Zaid ibn Aslam said: It was being raised for Idris every day the same amount of the deeds of all Adam's children, then an angel came to him in the form of a human being but Idris recognized him and asked him to let him test the death so that he can realize its strength and be very ready for it. God had inspired the angel to catch his soul for an hour then left it. Angel said: what did you see? He said it is harder than I was told but I would like that you let me see the Hell. The angel carried him to see it, then he said to the angel: "I would like to see the Heaven" the angel responded to him. When Idris was in the Heaven, the angel said to him: "come and get out of the Heaven" Idris said: "O Lord, I will not get out of it except God decides. The angel told God what happened God asked him: "What do you say", Idris said: 'Exalted is He says: "Every soul will taste death." " "كلُّ نَفْسٍ ذائِقَةُ المَوْتِ" (3:185) and I tasted it' and He says: "And there is none of you except he will come to it" "وَإِنْ مِنْكُمْ إِلاَّ وارِدُها" (19:71) and 'I came to the Hell' and He says: "Nor from it will they [ever] be removed." " "وَماهُمْ مِنها بِمُخْرَجِينَ" (15:48), then Idris said: "I will not get out except God gets me out. After that Idris listened to a call: "It is by my permission he gets in and goes so let him free."

History of Natioans (1)

Tale of events that had occurred during the era of Idris (PBUH)

The king of the whole world, then, was Puraceb; he was Zahak ibn Alahnoub, he was a friend for Satan, his religion was Brahmin. He was a king for all territories for about a thousand years.

Tale of events after Idris

Methuselah, son of Idris, was recommended by his Father before he was being raised to assume the call for God, he was the first one sailed in the sea and he was given the kingship because he obeyed God, Exalted is He.

Then, he had a son, Lamech, father of Noah (PBUH).

There were many events and centuries between the succession of Adam and Noah, most of them are unknown.

Some of those kings: King Tahmuras, he was descendant from Oching, he was a king for all territories, he built the place that King of Persians Shabour renewed, he is the first one to write in Persian language; he used horses, mules, donkeys and dogs to protect cattle.

Then, his brother Jamshid, succeeded him, he controlled the territories. He created swords and weapons. He commanded weaving and tinting the clothes. He classified people into four classes: the first for fighters, the second for writers, the third for manufacturers and ploughmen, and the fourth for servants and maids. He got out minerals from seas and mountains. Then, he became arrogant and ungrateful where he gathered all people and said to them that he was their king and the one who prevents them from oldness, sickness and death; he disregarded the favor of his Lord and claimed that he is a god.

It was said that a man became a king while he was young, he asked: "I did not find for the kingship a pleasure", people said to him: "The kingship has a pleasure", he said: "How can I get it?" It was said to him: "By obeying God". Then, he gathered the good people around him and asked them to be near to him in his assembly so that if they found an obedience, they shall ask him to do it, or if disobedience, ask him not to do it. So, he had been a king for 400 years obeying God.

Then, Satan paid attention to that, so he went to the king and said to him that he is Satan and asked him: "Who are you?", the king said: "I am a human being!", Satan said: "No, you are not. If you are a human being, you would die like people; did not you see how many people died and you are still alive! You are a god, invite people to worship you." He was charmed by this sweet words and he delivered a speech for his people and said: "I have concealed a matter; you know that I have been your king for 400 years, if I was a human being, I would die so long ago, but I am a god and you have to worship me". God had inspired some people to say to him that He was good for him as he was on the straight way to Me, if he diverts, He will send Nebuchadnezzar to kill him and take His properties.

CHAPTER 4

Tale of Noah (PBUH)

It is Noah ibn Lamech ibn Methuselah ibn Idris

Noah was born after 826 years of the death of Adam. When he grew up, his father told him only you and I who are on the right path, so do not feel strange and follow the sinful nation. Then, God sent him as a messenger for the people who worships idols to invite them to worship God but they were beating him much.

Scholars of biographies held that God imposed prayers, demonstrated lawful and unlawful matters, God commanded him to make a ship, so he planted a tree and when it was very big, he cut it to build the ship, his people were mocking him while they were passing by him. It was said that the tree had grown for 40 years and he made the ship during 400 years; its length was approximately 156 meters, its width was 26 meters and its height was 15 meters.

It was said that its length was 520 meters and it was three floors, a floor was for animals, the second for human beings and the third for birds.

It was said that human beings were 80; Sam, Ham, Japheth, his sons' wives and 73 children of Seth.

It was said that the reservoir was from stones. People differed regarding where was it? Some said it was in India and some said it was in Kufa.

It was narrated that when Noah got in the ship, Satan clung to the back of the ship. Noah said: "Who are you", He replied: "I am Satan." Noah said: "What do you want?" Satan said: "I came to ask your God, can I repent?" God had inspired Noah that his repentance comes true after prostrating before the grave of Adam. Satan said: "I did not prostrate for him while he was alive how I prostrate for him while he was dead?!" Exalted is He says: "He refused and was arrogant and became of the disbelievers." "أبى وَاسْتَكْبَرَ وَكانَ مِن الكافِرِينَ" (2:34).

Scholars said: When Noah resided on the ship, the gates of the heaven were opened with rain pouring down for forty days then the water covered the mountains and all creatures on Earth passed away.

The rain continued for forty days and forty nights, the beasts and the animals came to Noah, so that he to held a pair of each and held the body of Adam. The ship sailed for 6 months till it went around the earth, God raised Kaaba and the Black Stone, so as not to sink, then it stopped at the mountain of Judy in Iraq and it was said to the earth: "And it was said, "O earth, swallow your water, and O sky, withhold [your rain]."" وقيلَ يَاأَرْضُ ابْلَعِي مَاءَكِ "وَيَاسَمَاءُ أَقْلِعِي" (11:44).

Scholars said: Noah stayed in the ship till the water leveled down, then he took a piece of land to build a village, called Thamanin, each one had his house, it is still called Thamanin Market for today.

Scholars said: Noah lived after the flood for 350 years, total age of Noah 950 years and more. Noah had Sam, Ham, Japheth and Canaan, Exalted is He says: "And We made his descendants those remaining [on the earth]." "وَجَعَلْنَا ذُرِّيَّتَهُ هُمُ الْبَاقِينَ" (37:77). Some scholars said that all people are from the decedents of Noah.

Tale of Zahak King

He is Puraceb (The man who has 10000 horses). Some historians said that Noah was sent for this king and his people.

Most historians said he was the king of the seven territories and he was a magician and wicked. Zahak became a king after

History of Natioans (1)

Jim for 1000 years and his kingship was characterized with injustice and killing.

Persians claim that Zahak was a violator who disseized earth by his magic and he claimed that he was a prophet. People, then lived hard life till someone named Kabi who gathered people to stand against him, so Zahak fled and Fereydun assumed the kingship after him.

Fereydun became a king for 500 years while Zahak lived for 1000 years and was a king for 600 years. Some Persians say that Fereydun is Noah. Some people said that Fereydun is Dhulqarnayn and some said he is Solomon son of David.

Fereydun governed by justice and gave everyone his dues; he was the first to use elephants in the war. He was the king of earth, then he distributed it over his three sons; two of them killed the third, and they shared the earth and became kings for three hundred years. Then, Tawj ibn Fereydun oppressed, he had Afrasiab ibn Turk who is the ancestor of Turkmen.

Tale of Noah's sons (PBUH)

It was narrated that the Prophet (PBUH) said: "Sam was the father of Arabs, Ham the father of the Ethiopians, and Japheth the father of the Romans."

Tale of Sam's children

Sam's children: Fares, Tasem, Amliq, Aram and Arpachshad. Children of Arpachshad are prophets, messengers, righteous people, all Arabs and Pharaohs. Aram's children are 'Aber and 'Aws; children of 'Aber are Thamud and Gudais and children of 'Aws are 'Ad.

Tasem and Amliq speak Arabic; Fares speaks Persian.

'Aber begot Peleg; his grandson Terah, the father of Abraham. Also he begot Qahtan, the first king of Yemen, whose grandson is Sheba whose tribe is called after his name.

Ibn Abbas narrated that a man said: 'O Messenger of God! What is Sheba (Saba); is it a land or a woman?' He said: 'It is neither a land nor a woman, but it is a man who had ten sons among the Arabs. Six of them went south (in Yemen) and four of them went north (toward the Levant). As for those who went north, they are Lakhm, Judham, Ghassan and Amela. As for those who sent south, they are Azd, Al-'Ash'ariyyun, Himyar, Kindah, Madhhij, and Anmar.' A man said: 'O Messenger of God! Who are Anmar?' He said: 'Those among whom are Khath'am and Bajilah.'" [This Hadith has been said by Ibn 'Abbas reporting the Prophet (PBUH)].

Narrated Farwah ibn Musaik Almuradi: "I went to the Prophet (PBUH) and said: 'O Messenger of God! Shall I let the believers in my people fight those who turn away?! So he permitted me to fight them and made me their commander.' When I left him, he asked me, saying: 'What has Alghutaifi done?' He was informed that I set off on my journey." So he sent a message on my route that I should return. I went to him and he was with a group of his Companions. He said: 'Invite your people. Whoever accepts Islam is welcomed. And whoever does not accept Islam, do not be hasty until new news reaches you.'

Tale of Japheth's children

Some of his children are Jonah and his grandsons are the Romans. Also, all kings of non-Arabs like Turk, Persians and Khazars are all the children of Japheth.

Tale of Ham's children

One of them is Cush; his son is Nimrod, the first king 30 years after the Flood. His grandson is the king when the prophet Abraham is born. Also, Gog and Magog are his children.

• CHAPTER 5 •

Tale of events during the time between Noah and Abraham

Dividing earth by Noah's children:

Sam's children headed to a land between the Levant and Yemen, Ham's children moved to the south. Japheth's children traveled to the north. 'Ad moved to Shihr, 'Abl moved to Sanaa. Thamud traveled to Hegra (Mada'in Saleh), Tasem to Al-Yamama.

Event of worshipping idols After Noah:

Narrated ibn Abbas: All the idols which were worshiped by the people of Noah were worshiped by the Arabs later on. As for the idol Wadd, it was worshiped by the tribe of Kalb at Daumat-al-Jandal; Suwa' was the idol of (the tribe of) Hudhail; Yaghouth was worshiped by (the tribe of) Murad and then by Bani Ghutaif at Aljurf near Sheba; Ya'uq was the idol of Hamdan, and Nisr was the idol of Himyar, the branch of Dhi-al-Kala`. The names (of the idols) formerly belonged to some pious men of the people of Noah, and when they died, Satan inspired their people to prepare and place idols at the places where they used to sit, and to call those idols by their names. The people did so, but the idols were not worshiped till those people (who initiated them) had died and the origin of the idols had become obscure, whereupon people began worshiping them.

Event of tyranny of Aram's children; 'Ad And Thamud:

Tale of people of 'Ad and their atheism

When they became tyrants and worshipped idols, Exalted is He sent them Hud ibn Rabah ibn Alkholoud ibn 'Ad ibn 'Aws ibn Aram ibn Noah who invited them to monotheism and gave up injustice, they considered him liar and only very few who believed in Hud. They increased their tyranny saying: "They said, "It is all the same to us whether you advise or are not of the advisors." "سَوَاءٌ عَلَيْنَا أَوَعَظْتَ أَمْ لَمْ تَكُنْ مِنَ الْوَاعِظِينَ" (26:136). God prevent them rains for three years.

Exalted is He says: "And when they saw it as a cloud approaching their valleys, they said, "This is a cloud bringing us rain" "فَلَمَّا رَأَوْهُ عَارِضًا مُسْتَقْبِلَ أَوْدِيَتِهِمْ قَالُوا هَٰذَا عَارِضٌ مُمْطِرُنَا" (46:24). First one to see the cloud is a woman that cried seeing meteors of fire, Exalted is He says: "Which God imposed upon them for seven

nights and eight days in succession ".". "فسخرها الله عَلَيْهم سَبْعَ ليالٍ وَثَمانيَةَ
"أَيَّامٍ حُسُوماً" (69:7).

Tale of Luqman ibn 'Ad

Luqman, who lived for the age of seven eagles, was afflicted with women when he marries a woman, she betrays him. Scholars said that Hud lived for 15 years.

Tale of Thamud

They were insolent and disbelievers in God; they lived for longtime so they made houses in the mountains as their stone houses were demolished. God sent to them Salih, grandson of Thamud, after the destruction of people of 'Ad. They just increased tyranny after his invitation.

They asked him to give them a sign he said: "This is the she-camel of God [sent] to you as a sign. So leave her to eat within God's land and do not touch her with harm". "هَذِهِ نَاقَةُ اللَّـهِ لَكُمْ آيَةً فَذَرُوهَا تَأْكُلْ فِي أَرْضِ اللَّـهِ وَلَا تَمَسُّوهَا بِسُوءٍ" (7:73). The she-camel drinks their water for a day and they drink for a day, in return for they milk it. They intended to kill Salih but they were killed by a rock, then they hamstrung the she-camel. It was said that Salih stayed with his people for 20 years and he died in Mecca, while he was 58 years old and it was said that he lived for 270 years, and then God sent Abraham after him.

There was great prophet Daniel before Abraham and after Noah, yet the junior Daniel came in the era of Nebuchadnezzar..

• CHAPTER 6 •

Tale of Abraham (PBUH)

He is Abraham ibn Tareh ibn Nahor ibn Serug ibn Ragau ibn Peleg ibn Eber ibn Canaan ibn Sam ibn Noah.

Abraham was sent 3330 years after Adam and 1263 years after the Flood. Some scholars said that there was ten centuries between Noah and Abraham.

Scholars controverted regarding the place where he was born: most scholars agreed that he was born when Nimrod ibn Canaan... ibn Cush ibn Ham, governed the east and the west. Some scholars said that he was Zahak who wanted to burn Abraham.

The first king to dominate earth, east and west was Nimrod ibn Canaan. Scholars of biographies said: There were no prophets except Hud and Salih.

Astrologers said to Nimrud: there will be a boy in your village who will be born in a certain month, in a certain year, who will demolish your idols, he is named Abraham. Then, he slaughtered every boy was born in this year and month. When Abraham's mother, Amila was about to give birth to Abraham, she went to a cave and left him there and said to his father that the baby died. Abraham was growing rapidly, so when he started to talk, he told his mother to get him out. Amila told Azar about this incident, that pleased him.

Azar was making idols and was asking Abraham to sell them and Abraham says: "Who can buy what does not help or benefit?! So it was known amongst people that Abraham was mocking their idols. When they got out in a festival he said he was sick then he said: "I will surely plan against your idols"." "لَأَكِيدَنَّ أَصْنَامَكُمْ" (21:57). Some of them heard him, then he entered in the temple of the idols and offered them food and said: "Do not you eat?" and when he did not hear any voice he said: "Do not you talk?!" then he broke them and hanged the ax on the neck of the biggest of them,. When the people returned said: "Who has done this to our gods? "."مَن فَعَلَ هَذَا بِآلِهَتِنَا" (21:59). Some of them said: "We heard a young man mention them who is called Abraham"."سَمِعْنَا فَتًى يَذْكُرُهُمْ يُقَالُ لَهُ إِبْرَاهِيمُ" (21:60); He abused them. They took him to their king Nimrud who said: "Have you done this to our gods, O Abraham?"."قَالُوا أَأَنتَ فَعَلْتَ هَذَا بِآلِهَتِنَا يَا إِبْرَاهِيمُ" (21:62). Abraham said: "Rather, this - the largest of them - did it, so ask them, if they should [be able to] speak"."قَالَ بَلْ فَعَلَهُ

History of Natioans (1)

"كَبِيرُهُمْ هَٰذَا فَاسْأَلُوهُمْ إِن كَانُوا يَنطِقُونَ" (21:63). He was angry that those small idols were being worshipped together with him, so he broke them. Nimrud asked him: "What gods do you worship?" Abraham said: "My Lord is who gives life and causes death", Nimrud said: "I give life and cause death.", He got two men and said: "I can command his death so I cause him death and the other one I can forgive him so I give him life". Abraham said, "Indeed, God brings up the sun from the east, so bring it up from the west." So the disbeliever (Nimrud) was overwhelmed [by astonishment] and put him in jail for seven years.

Scholars narrated that Nimrud had two very hungry lions and that he sent to Abraham but they did not harm him and sat before him. Then, Nimrud and his people decided that they had to burn him.

Tale of throwing Abraham in Fire

Scholars said that Nimrud commanded collecting wood and they set the fire and they decided to throw him in it. Creatures said to God that no one on earth worships You except Abraham, allow us to help him. God said "If he asks help from anyone of you, help him and if he did not ask any one of you, I am his Ally." When he was thrown in fire, Exalted is He says: "O fire, be coolness and safety upon Abraham"."يَا نَارُ كُونِي بَرْدًا وَسَلَامًا عَلَىٰ إِبْرَاهِيمَ" (21:69). Gabriel came to Abraham and said "Do you want anything?" Abraham said: "From you, I do not." But Abraham said while he was in fire: "God will suffice me and He is the best Disposer of affairs".

Ibn Abbas said: "If the coolness is not followed by safety, Abraham would die." When fire was distinguished, they looked at Abraham and found with him another man who was wiping the face of Abraham, they got Abraham out of fire and went to the king. Some few people believed in Abraham when they saw this sign, Lot and Sara.

There were some events had occurred during Abraham time:

Abraham invited his father Azar to worship God, he said: "O my father, why do you worship that which neither hear, see nor benefit you at all?" His father said, "do not you desire my gods, O' Abraham? Azar disobeyed, so Abraham left him

Also, there were the migration of Abraham (PBUH):

Abraham and his companions (believers) agreed to leave their people and migrated with Lot and his wife Sara to Egypt. Abu Huraira narrated: The Prophet (PBUH) said, "The prophet Abraham (PBUH) emigrated with Sarah and entered a village where there was a king or a tyrant. (The king) was told that Abraham had entered (the village) accompanied by a woman who was one of the most charming women. So, the king sent for Abraham and asked, 'O Abraham! Who is this lady accompanying you?' Abraham replied, 'She is my sister (i.e. in religion).' Then Abraham returned to her and said, 'Do not contradict my statement, for I have informed them that you are my sister. By God, there are no true believers on this land except you and me.' Then Abraham sent her to the king. When the king got to her, she got up and performed ablution, prayed and said, 'O God! If I have believed in You and Your Apostle, and have saved my private parts from everybody except my husband, then please do not let this pagan overpower me.' Thereupon, the king fell in a mood of agitation and started moving his legs. Seeing the condition of the king, Sarah said, 'O God! If he should die, the people will say that I have killed him.' The king regained his power. The king got two or three attacks, and after recovering from the last attack he said, 'By God! You have sent a Satan to me. Take her to Abraham and give her Ajar.' So she came back to Abraham and said, 'God humiliated the pagan and gave us a slave-girl for service."

Hagar was beautiful maid, so Sarah granted her for Abraham and said "I find it beautiful, take her, may Lord bestow you a boy from her" She was barren. Then Abraham had married her, so Hagar became pregnant and gave birth to Ishmael.

Abraham got out of Egypt and went to the Levant; he stayed in Beersheba in Palestine while Lot stayed in overturned town.

From the events, also, Abraham went out to Mecca together with Gabriel. When they reached the place of enclosure and asked Hagar to build a lattice, then he went back to the Levant.

IBN AL-JAWZI

Ibn Abbas (May God be pleased with them) reported:

Ibrahim (PBUH) brought his wife and her son Ishmael (PBUH), while she was breastfeeding him, to a place near Kaaba under a tree on the spot of Zamzam, at the highest place in the mosque. In those days, there was no human being in Mecca, nor was there any water. So he made them sit over there and placed near them a leather bag containing some dates, and a small water-skin containing some water, and set out homeward. Ismail's mother followed him saying: "O Abraham! Where are you going, leaving us in this valley where there is no person whose company we may enjoy, nor is there anything (to enjoy)?" She repeated that to him many times, but he did not look back at her. Then she asked him: "Has God commanded you to do so?" He said: "Yes." She said: "Then He will not neglect us." She returned while Abraham proceeded onwards. Having reached the Thaniya, where they could not see him, he faced Kaaba, raised his both hands and supplicated: "Our Lord, I have settled some of my descendants in an uncultivated valley near Your sacred House, our Lord, that they may establish prayer. So make hearts among the people incline toward them and provide for them from the fruits that they might be grateful"." (14:37). "رَبَّنَا إِنِّي أَسْكَنتُ مِن ذُرِّيَّتِي بِوَادٍ غَيْرِ ذِي زَرْعٍ عِندَ بَيْتِكَ الْمُحَرَّمِ رَبَّنَا لِيُقِيمُوا الصَّلاَةَ فَاجْعَلْ أَفْئِدَةً مِّنَ النَّاسِ تَهْوِي إِلَيْهِمْ وَارْزُقْهُم مِّنَ الثَّمَرَاتِ لَعَلَّهُمْ يَشْكُرُونَ"

History of Natioans (1)

Ishmael's mother went on feeding Ishmael and drinking from the water which she had. When the water in the water-skin had all been used up, she became thirsty and her child also became thirsty. She started looking at Ishmael, tossing in agony. She left him, for she could not endure looking at him, and found that the mountain of As-Safa was the nearest mountain to her on that land. She stood on it and started looking at the valley keenly so that she might see somebody, but she could not see anybody. Then she descended from As-Safa, and when she reached the valley, she tucked up her robe and ran in the valley like a person in distress and trouble till she crossed the valley and reached Al-Marwah mountain where she stood and started looking, expecting to see somebody, but she could not see anybody. She repeated that (running between As-Safa and Al-Marwah) seven times."

Ibn Abbas further narrated: The Prophet (PBUH) said, "This is the source of the tradition of the Sa'y – (the going of people between the two mountains). When she reached Al-Marwah (for the last time), she heard a voice and she exclaimed: 'Shshs!' (Silencing herself) and listened attentively. She heard the voice again and said: 'O (whoever you may be) You have made me hear your voice; have you any succor for me?' And behold! She saw an angel at the place of Zamzam, digging the earth with his heel (or with his wing), till water flowed out from that place.

She started to make something like of a basin around it, using her hands in this way and began to fill her water-skin using her hands, and the water was flowing out until she had scooped some of it."

Ibn Abbas said: The Prophet (PBUH) further said, "May God bestow mercy on Ishmael's mother! Had she let Zamzam flow without trying to control it (or had she not scooped in that water) while filling her water-skin, Zamzam would have been a stream flowing on the surface of the earth." The Prophet (PBUH) further added, "Then she drank (water) and fed her child. The angel said to her: 'Do not be afraid of being neglected, for this is the site on which the House of God will be built by this boy and his father, and God will never let His believers neglected.' The House of God (the Kaaba) at that time was on a high place resembling a hillock, and when torrents came, they flowed to its right and left. She continued living in that way till some people from the tribe of Jurhum passed by her and her child. As they were coming from through the way of Kada', in the lower part of Mecca where they saw a bird that had a habit of flying around water and not leaving it. They said: 'This bird must be flying over water, though we know that there is no water in this valley.' They sent one or two messengers who discovered the source of water, and returned to inform them of the water existence. So, they all came towards the water." The Prophet (PBUH) added,

"Ishmael's mother was sitting near the water. They asked her: 'Do you allow us to stay with you?' She replied: 'Yes, but you will have no right to possess the water.' They agreed to that."

Ibn Abbas narrated that The Prophet (PBUH) further said, "Ishmael's mother was pleased with the whole situation as she used to love the company of the people. So, they settled there, and later on they called their families who came and settled with them. The child (i.e.: Ishmael) grew up and learnt Arabic from them, his virtues caused them to love and admire him as he grew up, and when he reached the age of puberty, they gave him one of their daughters in marriage. After Ishmael's mother had died, Ibrahim came after Ishmael's marriage in order to see his family that he had left before, but he did not find Ishmael there. When he asked Ishmael's wife about him, she replied: 'He has gone in search of our livelihood.' Then he asked her about their way of living and their condition, and she replied complaining to him: 'We are living in hardship, misery and destitution.' He said: 'When your husband returns, convey my salutations to him and tell him to change the threshold of the door of his house.' When Ishmael came, he seemed to have perceived something unusual.

He asked his wife: 'Did anyone visit you?' She replied: 'Yes, an old man of such and such description came and asked me about you and I informed him, and he asked about our state of living, and, I told him that we were living in hardship and poverty.' Thereupon Ishmael said: 'Did he advise you anything?' She replied: 'Yes, he told me to convey his salutations to you and to change the threshold of your door.' Ishmael said: 'That was my father, and he has ordered me to divorce you. Go back to your family.' So Ishmael divorced her and married another woman from amongst them (Jurhum). Then Ibrahim stayed away from them for a period as long as God wished, and called on them again but did not find Ishmael. So he came to Ishmael's wife and asked her about him. She said: 'He has gone in search of our livelihood.' Ibrahim asked her about their sustenance and living: 'How are you getting on?' She replied: 'We are prosperous and well off.' Then she praised God, the Exalted. Ibrahim asked: 'What kind of food do you eat?' She said: 'Meat.' He said: 'What do you drink?' She said: 'Water.' He said, 'O God! Bless their meat and water!'" The Prophet (PBUH) added, "At that time they did not have grain, and if they had grain, he would have also invoked God to bless it." The Prophet (PBUH) further said, "If somebody has only these two things as his sustenance, his health and disposition will be badly affected because these things do not suit him unless he lives in Mecca." The Prophet (PBUH) added, "Then Ibrahim said to Ishmael's wife, 'When your husband comes, give my regards to him and tell him that he should keep firm the threshold of his door.'

History of Natioans (1)

When Ishmael came back, he asked his wife: 'Did anyone call on you?' She replied: 'Yes, a good looking old man came to me.' She praised him and added: 'He asked about you, and I informed him, and he asked about our livelihood and I told him that we were in good condition.' Ishmael asked her: 'Did he give you a piece of advice?' She said: 'Yes, he told me to convey his regards to you and ordered that you should keep firm the threshold of your door.' On that Ishmael said: 'He was my father and you are the threshold of the door. He has ordered me to keep you with me.' Then Ibrahim stayed away from them for a period as long as God wished and called on them afterwards. He saw Ishmael under a tree near Zamzam, sharpening his arrows. When he saw Ibrahim, he rose up to welcome him, and they saluted each other as a father does with his son or a son does with his father. Ibrahim said: 'O Ishmael! God has given me an order.' Ishmael said: 'Do what your Lord has commanded you to do.' Ibrahim asked: 'Will you help me?' Ishmael said: 'I will help you.' Ibrahim said: 'God has ordered me to build a house here, pointing to a hillock higher than the land surrounding it.'" The Messenger of God (PBUH) added, "Then they raised the foundations of the House (i.e.: Kaaba). Ishmael brought the stones and Ibrahim was building (the house). When the walls became high, Ishmael brought stone and placed it for Ibrahim who stood over it and carried on building the House, while

Ishmael was handing over the stones to him, both of them prayed: "And [mention] when Abraham was raising the foundations of the House and [with him] Ishmael, [saying], "Our Lord, accept [this] from us. Indeed You are the Hearing, the Knowing." " وَإِذْ يَرْفَعُ إِبْرَاهِيمُ الْقَوَاعِدَ مِنَ الْبَيْتِ وَإِسْمَاعِيلُ رَبَّنَا تَقَبَّلْ مِنَّا إِنَّكَ أَنتَ السَّمِيعُ الْعَلِيمُ" (2:127).

One of events: God commands Abraham to build Kaaba.

Abraham(PBUH) visited Hagar and his son Ishmael three times after he came with them to Mecca and left them there, in the third time, he said to Ishmael that God commanded me to build Kaaba here. Abraham and his son built the Kaaba and while Ishmael was searching for a stone, he came to find that his father put the Black Stone in its place.

He asked his father: "Who fetch this stone for you?" Abraham said: "It was fetched by Gabriel from heaven. God inspired Abraham to build the Kaaba while he was 100 years old and his son was 30 years old. It was said that the Kaaba was built by Adam, then his children rebuilt it after him but the flood demolished it till it was built by Abraham and his son.

Borders of the Kaaba were set by Abraham after the commands of Gabriel, then Quraish moved these borders during the time of the Prophet (PBUH) where it was very hard for the Prophet. Gabriel came to him and said they would get them back. Some men of Quraish people dreamt that someone said to them that God honored them by this Kaaba and they moved its borders.

The Messenger of God (PBUH) sent a man in the year of the Conquest of Mecca Tamim ibn Rashid to renew it, then it was renewed by Omar ibn Alkhattab, Mo'awyah then Abdulmalek ibn Marawan.

Another event was When Abraham built the Kaaba; Exalted is He commanded him to call people for pilgrimage.

Ibn Abbas narrated: When the Kaaba was built, Exalted is He has revealed: "And proclaim to the people the Hajj [pilgrimage]"." "أذِّنْ في النَّاسِ بالحَجّ" (22:27). Abraham said: How far can my voice reach? God says: Proclaim to the pilgrimage and I will spread your word. Abraham called: "O people, your Lord has taken a house and commanded you to visit it." All creatures heard his voice and he answered: "I am at Your service; I am at Your service." All creatures, trees, dust and things responded: "I am at Your service; I am at Your service."

It was narrated by the Prophet (PBUH): "Gabriel came to Abraham on the Day of Satisfaction (The 8th day of Dhul-hijjah) and headed him to Mina, then he performed Dhuhr, Asr, Maghrib, 'Isha and Fajr prayers (Noontime, Afternoon, Sunset, Evening, Dawn, respectively) in Mina, then he went with him to Arafat Mount and they performed Dhuhr and Asr prayers together and so on, then it has revealed to Prophet Mohammed (PBUH) to follow the religion of Abraham.

Moreover, God has revealed ten scriptures to Abraham.

Abu Dharr said: I asked the prophet (PBUH) How many books have been revealed by God? He said: Hundred and four books, ten scriptures had been revealed to Adam, 50 scriptures to Seth, 30 scriptures to Idris and 10 scriptures to Abraham; and He revealed Torah, the Bible, Psalms and Quran.

Here it comes the event of Abraham becoming a friend of God.

Scholars differed regarding the reason; some said it was because he was always offering food and was very generous, others said it was because of breaking idols and arguing with them.

There was also the event when Abraham asked God to let him see how He gives life back to the dead?

Scholars differed regarding this question: one of them said it was because Abraham saw a corpse that the wild animals were eating; some said it was when he became a friend of God, so he asked this question so that he can be sure of the good tiding; others said he wanted to be sure and stop any doubts. An opinion referred to that was when he said: "My Lord is who gives life and causes death." He wanted to see what he told about his Lord.

Also, there was the event that God tested Abraham with commands and he fulfilled them. Scholars differ regarding these commands: some said that Abraham was tested by Islam, others said he was tested by purification, others said he was tested with pilgrimage rituals. An opinion referred that it was His saying, Exalted is He: "Indeed, I will make you a leader for the people"." (2:124) "إِنِّي جَاعِلُكَ لِلنَّاسِ إِمَامًا".

There was the event that God tested Abraham with sacrificing his son after performing pilgrimage.

Scholars differed regarding his son whether he was Ishmael or Isaac, some scholars narrated that the Prophet (PBUH) said: It was Isaac. Exalted is He says: "And We ransomed him with a great sacrifice"." "وَفَدَيْنَاهُ بِذِبْحٍ عَظِيمٍ" (37:107). Some scholars said it was not Isaac; they argued that God, Exalted is He, says: "And We gave him good tidings of Isaac"." "وَبَشَّرْنَاهُ بِإِسْحَاقَ" (37:112) after tale of sacrificing.

From these events is the event of Nimrod's end.

Upon Nimrod's refusal to obey and worship God, He sent him a mosquito that entered from his nose, as a result, he had beaten his head for 400 years. Nimrod had also built a tower to the heaven, Exalted is He says: "But God came at their building from the foundations, so the roof fell upon them from above them"." (16:26) "فَأَتَى اللَّـهُ بُنْيَانَهُم مِّنَ الْقَوَاعِدِ فَخَرَّ عَلَيْهِمُ السَّقْفُ مِن فَوْقِهِمْ".

Some of the events during Abraham time: Isaac was sent to the Levant, Ishmael was sent to Jurhum, Lot was sent to Sodom and Jacob was sent to earth of Canaan. Also, the end of Lot's people was one of the events that had occurred in the time of Abraham (PBUH).

People of Lot were people of adultery and sodomy. Scholars said: Lot invited his people to worship God and prohibited adultery but they refused and oppressed, he asked his Lord to punish them, Exalted is He sent Gabriel, Mikael and Israfil in the form of humans who visited Abraham. Abraham did not have guests for a time, he was so pleased with them so he offered them a calf but they refused to eat, they said: "We do not eat except after paying its price" Abraham said: "Its price is to mention the name of Lord before eating and praise to Lord after eating." Also, they did not eat, Abraham felt uneasy they might be thieves, they said to him: "Do not be afraid, we are sent to the people of Lot. Sarah laughed with joy: "How can you come to us and do not eat our food?", Gabriel said: "O' laugher, I tell you tidings that you are going to give birth to Isaac and Jacob", she was 90 years old and Abraham was 120 years old. When Abraham felt safe, he argued them regarding the people of Lot, Exalted is He says: "And when the fright had left Abraham and the good tidings had reached him, he began to argue with Us

concerning the people of Lot"." فَلَمَّا ذَهَبَ عَنْ إِبْرَاهِيمَ الرَّوْعُ وَجَاءَتْهُ الْبُشْرَىٰ
"يُجَادِلُنَا فِي قَوْمِ لُوطٍ" (11:47). He argued with them since they said: "They said, "Indeed, we will destroy the people of that Lot's city. Indeed, its people have been wrongdoers"." قَالُوا إِنَّا مُهْلِكُو أَهْلِ هَٰذِهِ الْقَرْيَةِ إِنَّ أَهْلَهَا كَانُوا ظَالِمِينَ" (29:31).

They went to Lot and said: "We are your guests tonight", he said: "Do you know what the people of this village do? no people on earth are worse than them." Lot's people prevent him to have any guest so he took them to his house secretly, only his family knows, but his wife went out to her people and told them, so they went to him in hast. When his people came to him, he asked them not to disgrace him and said: "O my people, these are my daughters; they are purer for you. So fear God and do not disgrace me concerning my guests. Is there not among you a man of reason?"." قَالَ يَا قَوْمِ هَٰؤُلَاءِ بَنَاتِي هُنَّ أَطْهَرُ لَكُمْ فَاتَّقُوا اللَّهَ وَلَا تُخْزُونِ فِي ضَيْفِي أَلَيْسَ مِنْكُمْ رَجُلٌ رَشِيدٌ" (11:78). They said: "You have already known that we have not concerning your daughters any claim, and indeed, you know what we want"." لَقَدْ عَلِمْتَ مَا لَنَا فِي بَنَاتِكَ مِنْ حَقٍّ وَإِنَّكَ لَتَعْلَمُ مَا نُرِيدُ" (11:79). They did not think about what he said, so Lot said: "If only I had against you some power or could take refuge in a strong support"." لَوْ أَنَّ لِي بِكُمْ قُوَّةً أَوْ آوِي إِلَىٰ رُكْنٍ شَدِيدٍ" (11:80). The angels said, "O Lot, indeed we are messengers of your Lord; [therefore], they will never reach you. Lot said: "Demolish them all", Gabriel said: "Indeed, their appointment is

[for] the morning. Is not the morning near?" They said: "So set out with your family during a portion of the night and let not any among you look back - except your wife; indeed, she will be struck by that which strikes them. Exalted is He says: "So when Our command came, We made the highest part [of the city] its lowest and rained upon them stones of layered hard clay, [which were] Marked from your Lord. And God's punishment is not from the wrongdoers [very] far"." فلمَّا جَاءَ أَمْرُنَا جَعَلْنَا عَالِيَهَا سَافِلَهَا وَأَمْطَرْنَا (11:82- "عَلَيْهَا حِجَارَةً مِّن سِجِّيلٍ مَّنضُودٍ. مُّسَوَّمَةً عِندَ رَبِّكَ وَمَا هِيَ مِنَ الظَّالِمِينَ بِبَعِيدٍ 83). Lot died when he was 80 years old, before the death of Abraham.

Also, Sarah died during the time of Abraham.

She died in the Levant; it was said she died in Canaan land when she was 127 years old. Hagar died in Mecca before building the Kaaba. Abraham got married to a woman from Canaan, she was called Keturah, after Sarah had died. Keturah gave birth to 6 children: one of them was Midian and his other children to whom Shuaib was sent.

It was said that Dhulqarnayn lived during the time of Abraham. It was narrated by ibn Abbas that Dhulqarnayn had met Abraham in Mecca.

Scholars differed regarding whether Dhulqarnayn was a prophet or not. Some said he was a prophet but many scholars disagreed and said he was a pious man who commanded his people to be pious to God. Some said that he was a king. Scholars differed regarding his name; it was narrated that he was so-named because he went to east and west of earth carried by clouds because he was a pious and obedient to God.

Also, it was narrated that he was so-called because he was the king of Persians and Romans. It was narrated that he lived for more than two centuries (Qarnayn means two centuries in Arabic). It was said that the whole earth was governed by four kings: Two are believers and the others are disbelievers; the two believers are Solomon, son of David and Dhulqarnayn but the disbelievers are Nimrod and Nebuchadnezzar. It was said that Dhulqarnayn was one of the greatest kings of earth where God bestowed him monotheism, obedience and reasons of good; and helped him against his enemies, conquering cities and forts. He lived for a long time, he reached the east and west, he built the dam between people and Gog and Magog and he was a mercy for the believers.

His Tale

It was said that the Prophet (PBUH) said: "He was a young man from Romans who inherited a kingdom and went to Egypt and built a city named Alexandria". He walked till he reached the west of earth (sunset), he found a people there. God said to him: "O' Dhul-Qarnayn, either you punish [them] or else adopt among them [a way of] goodness." He said: "As for one who wrongs, we will punish him. Then he will be returned to his Lord, and He will punish him terribly. But as for one who believes and does righteousness, he will have a reward of Paradise, and we will speak to him with ease.

When he came to the rising of the sun, he found it rising on a people against whom no shield exists, then he followed his way until when he reached [a pass] between two mountains, he found beside them a people who could hardly understand [his] speech. They said, "O' Dhulqarnayn, indeed Gog and Magog are [great] corrupters in the land. So may we assign for you an expenditure that you might make between us and them a barrier?", He said: "That which my Lord has established me is better [than what you offer], but assist me with strength; I will make between you and them a dam. Bring me sheets of iron" - when he had leveled [them] between the two mountain walls, he said, "Blow [with bellows]," until he had made it [like] fire, he said, "Bring me, that I may pour over it molten copper." So Gog and Magog were unable to pass over it, nor were they able [to effect] in it any penetration.

It was narrated by Abu Hurairah that the Messenger of God (PBUH) said:

"Gog and Magog people dig every day until they can almost see the rays of the sun, the one in charge of them says: "Go back and we will dig it tomorrow." Then God puts it back, stronger than it was before. (This will continue) until their time has come, and God wants to send them against the people, they will dig until they can almost see the rays of the sun, then the one who is in charge of them will say: "Go back, and we will dig it tomorrow if God wills.' So they will say: "If God wills." Then they will come back to it and it will be as they left it. So they will dig and will come out to the people, and they will drink all the water. The people will fortify themselves against them in their forts. They will shoot their arrows towards the sky and they will come back with blood on them, and they will say: "We have defeated the people of earth and dominated the people of heaven." Then God will send a worm in the napes of their necks and will kill them thereby." The Messenger of God (PBUH) said: "By the One in Whose Hand is my soul, the beasts of the earth will grow fat on your flesh."

It was narrated by Alnawwas ibn Samaan, who said that the Messenger of God said: "The Muslims will burn their bows, arrows and quivers for seventy years."

Tale of his death

It was said that when Dhulqarnayn reached to the setting and the rise of the sun, he went to Babylon and was very sick, then he died (May God's mercy be upon him). Scholars differed regarding his age; they said that he lived for 3000 years, some said he lived for 1600 years.

CHAPTER 7

Event of Abraham's death (PBUH)

When God wanted to seize the soul of Abraham, he commanded the Death Angel to be lenient. Abraham's age was estimated to be 200 years and some people said it was 175 years and he was buried next to the grave of Sarah.

Tale of Ishmael

Ishmael is the eldest son of Abraham's children, he was born when his father was 90 years old; Isaac was born 30 years after. It is previously mentioned that Sarah gave Hagar for Abraham to be his maid and she gave birth of Ishmael, Abraham migrated with Hagar to Mecca and he got Ishmael married to a woman from Jurhum.

Ishmael had birth of twelve children. God took Ishmael as a prophet when he was sent to 'Amaliq, Jurhum and Yemen tribes where he prohibited worshipping idols, only few people believed in him but many disbelieve him. Hagar died when Ismael was 20 years and she was then 90 years old.

It was said that Ishmael is the first one to talk Arabic when he was 13 years old. Scholars said: Ishmael entrusted his brother Isaac and his son, he lived 137 years and he was buried next to his mother Hagar.

Tale of Isaac (PBUH)

It was said that Abraham did not die except after sending Isaac to the Levant, Jacob ibn Isaac to Canaan, Ishmael to Jurhum and Lot to Sodom; they were all alive during the life of Abraham. Abraham got Isaac married to Rebecca who gave birth of Esau and Jacob. Esau got married to the daughter of his uncle Ishmael who got birth of Romans. His children were many so that they dominated Canaan's people in the Levant.

Scholars said: Isaac lived for 16 years and he died in Palestine. He was buried next to his father's grave, then the kingship was transferred to the children of Isaac.

Tale of Jacob (PBUH)

It is previously mentioned that Jacob was born and became a prophet during the life of Abraham. Scholars said that Isaac preferred Jacob, so Esau hated Jacob and wanted to kill him, so Jacob fled to his uncle who got him married to Leah who gave birth to Reuben, Simeon, Levi, Issachar, Zebulun and Judah then she died. Then he married her sister Rachel who gave birth to Joseph and Benjamin.

People of the Book said: they were prophets where Reuben is the eldest brother; then Simeon; Judah, David and Jesus were from the children of Judah; then Levi, Moses and Aaron were from his children; then, Issachar; then, Zebulun; Gad; Asher; Dan; Naphtali; then Joseph and Benjamin. Mother of Reuben, Simeon, Levi, Judah, Zebulun and Issachar was Leah, daughter of Laban, Uncle of Jacob; they had a sister from Jacob called Dinah, the wife of Job. The mother of Asher and Gad was called Bilhah. Rachel was the mother of Joseph and Benjamin and the sister of Leah, daughters of Laban.

Tale of Joseph is one of the events that occurred during the life of Jacob.

Scholars said: When Joseph's brothers saw the great love of Jacob to Joseph and knew about the dream and that the sun and the moon prostrating to him, they envied him.

The siblings said: "Joseph and his brother are more beloved to our father than us, while we are a clan." They said to Jacob: "Send him with us tomorrow that he may eat well and play. And indeed, we will be his guardians. Jacob said: "Indeed, it saddens me that you should take him, and I fear that a wolf would eat him while you are unaware of him." When they went out to the wild land, they started to beat him. They throw him into the bottom of the well and while they were trying to kill him, Judah said to them you promised me not to kill him. Then they came to their father at night, weeping and said: "O' our father, indeed we went racing each other and left Joseph with our possessions, and a wolf ate him."; they brought upon his shirt false blood of a small goat. After three days came a company of travelers, they sent their water drawer, and they let down their bucket. They said: "Good news! Here is a boy." His brothers said he was a bad boy and sell him for 20 Dirhams, then they sold him in Egypt where Potiphar, the captain of the palace guard in Egypt, the treasurer, bought him and went to his wife Zulaikha and told: "Make his residence comfortable. Perhaps he will benefit us, or we will adopt him as a son." Joseph has not been in a relation with women, so Zulaikha sought to seduce him; she closed the doors and said: "Come, you"." هَيْتَ لَكَ" (12:23), he said: "[I seek] the refuge of God"." مَعَاذَ الله"(12:23).

The witness who delivered his testimony was a baby.

Scholars said: A witness from her family testified. "If his shirt is torn from the front, then she has told the truth, and he is of the liars. But if his shirt is torn from the back, then she has lied, and he is of the truthful." When Potiphar saw that his shirt was torn from the back, he said: "Indeed, it is of the women's plan. Indeed, your plan is great"." إِنَّهُ مِن كَيْدِكُنَّ إِنَّ كَيْدَكُنَّ عَظِيمٌ" (12:28), then he said: "Joseph, ignore this. And, [my wife], ask forgiveness for your sin. Indeed, you were of the sinful"." يُوسُفُ اعْرِضْ عَنْ هَذَا وَاسْتَغْفِرِي لِذَنبِكِ إِنَّكِ كُنتِ مِنَ الْخَاطِئِينَ" (12:29). The event became familiar so the women said: "The wife of Al'azeez is seeking to seduce her slave boy; he has impassioned her with love. Indeed, we see her [to be] in clear error"." امْرَأَتُ الْعَزِيزِ تُرَاوِدُ "فَتَاهَا عَن نَّفْسِهِ قَدْ شَغَفَهَا حُبًّا إِنَّا لَنَرَاهَا فِي ضَلَالٍ مُّبِينٍ (12:30). When she heard that she prepared them a banquet and pillows and gave each one of them a knife and said [to Joseph]: "Come out before them". When they saw him: "They greatly admired him and cut their hands and said, "Perfect is God! This is not a man; this is none but a noble angel"." أَكْبَرْنَهُ وَقَطَّعْنَ أَيْدِيَهُنَّ وَقُلْنَ حَاشَ لِلَّهِ مَا هَذَا بَشَرًا إِنْ هَذَا إِلَّا "مَلَكٌ كَرِيمٌ" (12:31). Then she said: "That is the one about whom you blamed me. And I certainly sought to seduce him, but he firmly refused; and if he will not do what I order him, he will surely be imprisoned and will be of those debased"." فَذَلِكُنَّ الَّذِي "لُمْتُنَّنِي فِيهِ وَلَقَدْ رَاوَدتُّهُ عَن نَّفْسِهِ فَاسْتَعْصَمَ وَلَئِن لَّمْ يَفْعَلْ مَا آمُرُهُ لَيُسْجَنَنَّ (12:32). Joseph said: "My Lord, prison is more to my liking than that to which they invite me"." رَبِّ السِّجْنُ أَحَبُّ إِلَيَّ مِمَّا يَدْعُونَنِي إِلَيْهِ" (12:33). She said to her husband that this slave disgraces her, and he has to imprison him so, he did. There entered the prison with him two young men; they were servants to the king; one of them was who is responsible for the food and the other for the drinks. Joseph said while he was in prison that he can inform about the interpretation of the dreams. One of them said, "Indeed, I have seen myself [in a dream] pressing wine." The other said, "Indeed, I have seen myself carrying upon my head [some] bread, from which the birds were eating. Inform us of its interpretation". Joseph informed them about their dreams and he invited them to monotheism by saying: "Are separate lords better or God, the One, the Prevailing?"." أَأَرْبَابٌ مُّتَفَرِّقُونَ خَيْرٌ أَمِ اللَّـهُ الْوَاحِدُ الْقَهَّارُ" (12:39). Joseph said to the one whom he knew that he would go free: "Mention me before your master"."اذْكُرْنِي عِندَ رَبِّكَ" (12:42), that I was put in prison unjustly.

But Satan made Joseph forget the mention [to] his Master, Joseph wept and asked for forgiveness of his Lord, so Joseph remained in prison seven years. Then the king saw a vision: "Indeed, I have seen [in a dream] seven fat cows being eaten by seven [that were] lean, and seven green spikes [of grain] and others [that were] dry"." إِنِّي أَرَىٰ سَبْعَ بَقَرَاتٍ سِمَانٍ يَأْكُلُهُنَّ سَبْعٌ عِجَافٌ وَسَبْعَ سُنبُلَاتٍ خُضْرٍ وَأُخَرَ يَابِسَاتٍ" (12:43). He told it to the close ones, explain to me my vision, if you should interpret visions. They said: "[It is but] a mixture of false dreams, and we are not learned in the interpretation of dreams"." أَضْغَاثُ أَحْلَامٍ وَمَا نَحْنُ بِتَأْوِيلِ الْأَحْلَامِ بِعَالِمِينَ" (12:44). One of the two young men who was freed said: "I will inform you of its interpretation, so send me forth."; he remembered the state of Joseph, they sent him and when he came to Joseph, he told him about the vision, Joseph said: "You will plant for seven years consecutively; and what you harvest leave in its spikes, except a little from which you will eat. Then will come after that seven difficult [years] which will consume what you saved for them, except a little from which you will store. Then will come after that a year in which the people will be given rain and in which they will press [olives and grapes]"." تَزْرَعُونَ سَبْعَ سِنِينَ دَأَبًا فَمَا حَصَدتُّمْ فَذَرُوهُ فِي سُنبُلِهِ إِلَّا قَلِيلًا مِّمَّا تَأْكُلُونَ. ثُمَّ يَأْتِي مِن بَعْدِ ذَٰلِكَ سَبْعٌ شِدَادٌ يَأْكُلْنَ مَا قَدَّمْتُمْ لَهُنَّ إِلَّا قَلِيلًا مِّمَّا تُحْصِنُونَ، ثُمَّ يَأْتِي مِن بَعْدِ ذَٰلِكَ عَامٌ فِيهِ يُغَاثُ النَّاسُ وَفِيهِ يَعْصِرُونَ." (12:47-49). The young man went back to the king and told him, the king said: "Bring him to me"." ائْتُونِي بِهِ"(12:50). Then, Joseph refused to get out of prison and said: "Return to your master and ask him what is the case of the women who cut their hands"." "مَا بَالُ النِّسْوَةِ اللَّاتِي قَطَّعْنَ أَيْدِيَهُنَّ"(12:50). The king Said to the women: "What was your condition when you sought to seduce Joseph?" They said, "Perfect is God! We know about him no evil"." مَا خَطْبُكُنَّ إِذْ رَاوَدتُّنَّ يُوسُفَ عَن نَّفْسِهِ قُلْنَ حَاشَ لِلَّهِ مَا عَلِمْنَا عَلَيْهِ مِن سُوءٍ" (12:51). But the wife of Al'azeez said: "Now the truth has become evident. It was I who sought to seduce him, and indeed, he is of the truthful"." الْآنَ حَصْحَصَ الْحَقُّ أَنَا رَاوَدتُّهُ عَن نَّفْسِهِ وَإِنَّهُ لَمِنَ الصَّادِقِينَ" (12:51). By this matter, Joseph intended that Al'azeez will know that he did not betray him in [his] absence.

When it was clear the honesty and innocence of Joseph, he said: "Bring him to me; I will appoint him exclusively for myself"." "ائْتُونِي بِهِ أَسْتَخْلِصْهُ لِنَفْسِي" (12:54). And when he came to him, the king said: "Indeed, you are today established [in position] and trusted". "إِنَّكَ الْيَوْمَ لَدَيْنَا مَكِينٌ أَمِينٌ" (12:54). Joseph said: "Appoint me over the storehouses of the land. Indeed, I will be a knowing guardian"." "اجْعَلْنِي عَلَىٰ خَزَائِنِ الْأَرْضِ إِنِّي حَفِيظٌ عَلِيمٌ" (12:55). He aimed to control keeping food and as he was very aware. The king entrusted him the position of Potiphar whom he died after that.

When Joseph assumed the rule, he ordered people to plant and leave the wheat in its ears, then the barren years came true and Palestine became arid. Zuleikha was changed after years and she became blind. She sat on the road waiting for Joseph. When he passes before her, she calls him but he did not hear her voice. Once, she said: "O Al'azeez, Exalted is he when he made slaves kings by obedience and made kings slaves by disobedience." Joseph heard her and wept, then turned to her and said: "Who are you, old lady?" She said: I am Zuleikha." Joseph said: "You can ask me to do three things for you" she said: "Ask your God to give me back my sight and youth" He called God for this, so she became young and beautiful, then she asked him to ask his God to be very beautiful again, so he did; she became a girl at age of 18 years. She asked him her third request that he marries her. God inspired him to marry her and they had birth to 12 children. Canaan land became arid and the cattle of Jacob died. Jacob and his children starved, so he told them to go to 'Azeez of Egypt to buy food. Joseph told the men on the gates that when any people come from the Levant, they have to ask them about their state and story. When Jacob's children came to Egypt, they were asked: "Where are you from?" They said we are Canaans; we are children of the prophet Jacob, the guards sent to Joseph these news.

Joseph let them meet him; "And the brothers of Joseph came [seeking food], and they entered upon him; and he recognized them, but he was to them unknown"." وَجَاءَ إِخْوَةُ يُوسُفَ فَدَخَلُوا عَلَيْهِ "فعَرَفَهُمْ وَهُمْ لَهُ مُنكِرُونَ" (12:59). Joseph asked them: "Who are you?" They introduced themselves. When they were about to leave, he asked them: How do you find my personality and generosity? They said: May God rewards you good. Joseph asked them: "How many children of Jacob? They said: "We are twelve brothers." Joseph said: "Why do I see 10 only?" They said: "One of them is called Joseph and the wolf eats him and the second one is at the service of our father." Joseph said: "Come with this brother or I will not sell you": " But if you do not bring him to me, no measure will there be [hereafter] for you from me, nor will you approach me"." "فإِن لَمْ تَأْتُونِي بِهِ فَلَا كَيْلَ لَكُمْ عِندِي وَلَا تَقْرَبُونِ" (12:60).

They went back to Jacob and told him the story, Jacob wept and said: "Should I entrust you with him except [under coercion] as I entrusted you with his brother before? But God is the best guardian, and He is the most merciful of the merciful"." هَلْ آمَنُكُمْ

(12:64). "عَلَيْهِ إِلَّا كَمَا أَمِنتُكُمْ عَلَىٰ أَخِيهِ مِن قَبْلُ ۖ فَاللَّهُ خَيْرٌ حَافِظًا ۖ وَهُوَ أَرْحَمُ الرَّاحِمِينَ"
When they opened their baggage, they found their merchandise returned to them; they said: "O our father, what [more] could we desire? This is our merchandise returned to us. And we will obtain supplies for our family and protect our brother and obtain an increase of a camel's load; that is an easy measurement"." "يَا أَبَانَا مَا نَبْغِي ۖ هَٰذِهِ بِضَاعَتُنَا رُدَّتْ إِلَيْنَا ۖ وَنَمِيرُ أَهْلَنَا وَنَحْفَظُ أَخَانَا وَنَزْدَادُ كَيْلَ بَعِيرٍ ۖ ذَٰلِكَ كَيْلٌ يَسِيرٌ" (12:65). They continued persuading Jacob till he agreed and said: "O my sons, do not enter from one gate but enter from different gates"." "يَا بَنِيَّ لَا تَدْخُلُوا مِن بَابٍ وَاحِدٍ وَادْخُلُوا مِنْ أَبْوَابٍ مُتَفَرِّقَةٍ" (12:67), to avoid being envied.

While they were having food with Joseph, he commanded putting the bowl (in gold) in the bag of his brother Benjamin and when they went out, Then an announcer called out: "O caravan, indeed you are thieves"." "أَيَّتُهَا الْعِيرُ إِنَّكُمْ لَسَارِقُونَ" (12:70). They said while approaching them, "What is you are missing?" The announcer said: "We are missing the measure of the king. And for he who produces it is [the reward of] a camel's load." They said, "By God, you have certainly known that we did not come to cause corruption in the land, and we have not been thieves." The accusers said, "Then what would be its recompense if you should be liars?" [The brothers] said, "In whose bag it is found - he [himself] will be the recompense." The bowl was put in the Benjamin's bag, whom Joseph wanted to have him. The eldest one of them Reuben, said: "Do you not know that your father has taken upon you an oath by God and [that] before you failed in [your duty to] Joseph? So I will never leave [this] land until my father permits me or God decides for me"." تَعْلَمُوا أَنَّ أَبَاكُمْ قَدْ أَخَذَ عَلَيْكُم مَّوْثِقًا مِّنَ اللَّـهِ وَمِن قَبْلُ مَا فَرَّطتُمْ فِي يُوسُفَ فَلَنْ أَبْرَحَ الْأَرْضَ حَتَّىٰ يَأْذَنَ لِي أَبِي أَوْ يَحْكُمَ اللَّـهُ لِي" (12:80). When they told Jacob, he said: "Perhaps God will bring them to me all together. Indeed it is He who is the Knowing, the Wise"." عَسَى اللَّـهُ أَن يَأْتِيَنِي بِهِمْ جَمِيعًا إِنَّهُ هُوَ الْعَلِيمُ الْحَكِيمُ" (12:83). He turned away from them and said, "Oh, my sorrow over Joseph," and his eyes became white from grief. They said: "By God, you will not cease remembering Joseph until you become fatally ill or become of those who perish"." تَاللَّـهِ تَفْتَأُ تَذْكُرُ يُوسُفَ حَتَّىٰ تَكُونَ حَرَضًا أَوْ تَكُونَ مِنَ الْهَالِكِينَ" (12:85). He said, "I only complain of my suffering and my grief to God, and I know from God that which you do not know." Jacob asked them to get back to Egypt: "O my sons, go and find out about Joseph and his brother and despair not of relief from God"." يَا بَنِيَّ اذْهَبُوا فَتَحَسَّسُوا مِن يُوسُفَ وَأَخِيهِ وَلَا تَيْأَسُوا مِن رَّوْحِ اللَّـهِ" (12:87).

They went back to Egypt and met Joseph saying: "O Al'azeez, adversity has touched us and our family, and we have come with goods poor in quality, but give us full measure and be charitable to us"." يَا أَيُّهَا الْعَزِيزُ مَسَّنَا وَأَهْلَنَا الضُّرُّ وَجِئْنَا بِبِضَاعَةٍ مُّزْجَاةٍ فَأَوْفِ لَنَا الْكَيْلَ وَتَصَدَّقْ عَلَيْنَا" (12:88). Joseph said to them: "Do you know

هَلْ عَلِمْتُم مَّا فَعَلْتُم بِيُوسُفَ "what you did with Joseph and his brother"." "وَأَخِيهِ" (12:89).

They said, "Are you indeed Joseph?" He said: "I am Joseph, and this is my brother. God has certainly favored us"." أَنَا يُوسُفُ "وَهَـٰذَا أَخِي قَدْ مَنَّ اللَّـهُ عَلَيْنَا" (12:90). They said, "By God, certainly has God preferred you over us"."تَاللَّـهِ لَقَدْ آثَرَكَ اللَّـهُ عَلَيْنَا"(12:91). Joseph asked about his father, they said that he became blind because of much weeping. Joseph said to them: "Take this, my shirt, and cast it over the face of my father; he will become seeing. And bring me your family, all together"." اذْهَبُوا بِقَمِيصِي هَـٰذَا فَأَلْقُوهُ عَلَىٰ وَجْهِ "أبي يَأْتِ بَصِيرًا وَأْتُونِي بِأَهْلِكُمْ أَجْمَعِينَ" (12:93). When they departed Jacob said: "And when the caravan departed [from Egypt], their father said, "Indeed, I find the smell of Joseph [and would say that he was alive] if you did not think me weakened in mind"." وَلَمَّا فَصَلَتِ "العِيرُ قَالَ أَبُوهُمْ إِنِّي لَأَجِدُ رِيحَ يُوسُفَ لَوْلَا أَن تُفَنِّدُونِ" (12:94). Judah was who gave previously his father the shirt with blood of Joseph and said that the wolf ate him and he also was the son who gave his father the shirt of Joseph and said he was still alive, he cast it over his face, and he returned [once again] seeing. They said, "O our father, ask for us forgiveness from our sins; indeed, we have been sinners"." "يَا أَبَانَا اسْتَغْفِرْ لَنَا ذُنُوبَنَا إِنَّا كُنَّا خَاطِئِينَ" (12:97). He said, "I will ask forgiveness for you from my Lord"."سَوْفَ أَسْتَغْفِرُ لَكُمْ رَبِّي" (12:98).

History of Natioans (1)

Jacob, his children and his people entered Egypt while Joseph went out to meet them; he took his parents to himself and said, "Enter Egypt, God willing, safe [and secure]." He raised his parents upon the throne, and they bowed to him in prostration.

Joseph said: "O my father, this is the explanation of my vision of before. My Lord has made it reality"." يَا أَبَتِ هَٰذَا تَأْوِيلُ رُؤْيَايَ مِن قَبْلُ قَدْ جَعَلَهَا رَبِّي حَقًّا"(12:100). Scholars said that there were 40 years between the vision and its explanation, some scholars said it was 80 years; He was 17 when he was thrown in the well and after 80 years he met his father and he lived for 23 years after that; he died while he was 120 years old.

Some scholars said that Jacob lived in Egypt for 24 years with Joseph and some said it was 17 years; Jacob died at the age of 147 years old. He was buried next to his father Isaac and also Joseph was buried next to them..

.

CHAPTER 8

Tale of Job (PBUH)

He was Job ibn Amous ibn Razih ibn Esau ibn Isaac ibn Abraham.

A scholar said that Job lived during Jacob's era (PBUH); he married to the daughter of Jacob and his mother was the daughter of Lot (PBUH).

Some scholars said that Job was after Solomon and some said after Jonah.

He lived in the Levant, he was rich and generous; he was known for his hospitality and giving alms. Satan was very envied because Job was very mentioned among the angels. He said to God If you tested Job, he would disbelieve, God said: Go I permit you to dominate his property, children and his body.

Job was the first one to be infected with smallpox. Satan commanded his soldiers to afflict him with disasters and afflictions. His children died all while they were eating when a strong wind hit the house they were in.

While he was in those bad afflictions, his wife told him to ask his Lord to heal him, he said we were in good time for seventy years and we have to endure the affliction and be patient for seventy years. He told his Lord, "Indeed, Satan has touched me with hardship and torment." While he was in this bad affliction, God sent Gabriel who hold his hands and said to him stand up, he stood. Then Gabriel said to him: 'Run' he ran. Then, Gabriel put him on a garment from the Heaven. He was asked to strike the ground with his foot, there was a spring for a cool bath and drink. God had given back his property and children, as a mercy because he was patient and an excellent servant.

Narrated Abu Huraira: The Prophet (PBUH) said, "When Prophet Job (Aiyub) (PBUH) was taking a bath naked, golden locusts began to fall on him. Job started collecting them in his clothes. His Lord addressed him, 'O Job! Haven't I given you enough so that you are not in need of them.' Job replied, 'Yes!' By Your Honor (power)! But I cannot dispense with Your Blessings."

Scholars said: Job was 73 years old and some said he was 93 years old but some said that he lived for 146 years.

Section Tale of Shuaib (PBUH)

Shuaib ibn 'Iefa ibn Nuwayb ibn Midian ibn Abraham.

History of Natioans (1)

Some scholars said he was not from the children of Abraham he was the child of the daughter of Lot.

He was sent to two nations: People of Midian and Companions of Wood. Scholars said he was sent to the people of Midian while he was 20 years old; they were people who gave less than due regarding measure or weight. He said to them: "Fear He who created you and the former creation." They said: "You are but a man like ourselves, and indeed, we think you are among the liars." And said: "So cause to fall upon us fragments of the sky, if you should be of the truthful." They denied him, so the punishment of the day of the black cloud seized them. Indeed, it was the punishment of a terrible day. It was a very hot day and God sent them a cloud where they gathered under it because of its coldness till they all gathered under it, then God sent them a fire that burnt them all.

Then, Shuaib stayed with the Companions of the Wood the rest of his life inviting them to worship God, Exalted is He, and commanded them to believe in God and in His books and messengers. They said, "O Shuaib, we do not understand much of what you say, and indeed, we consider you among us as weak", Some scholars said that he was blind when he was old, "And if not for your family, we would have stoned you [to death]; and you are not to us one respected." They denied the messengers and Shuaib's invitation to them increased them tyranny. People of Midian was tortured by the shriek (Blast) seized them at early morning. But the Companions of Wood were tortured by hot weather for seven days, then God had sent them a fire that burnt them all.

Shuaib's daughter got married to Moses and he appointed Moses after him, then he went to Mecca till he died there. He was buried in the House near to the Black Stone.

Events that happened during the time of Shuaib

One of these events is the rule of the king Manuchehr ibn Iraj ibn Fereydun. When he became an adult, his grandfather appointed him, as the king after him. Moses was sent 60 years after the beginning of his rule and he stayed another 60 years ruling till there was an enemy that expatriated him for 12 years. Then, he managed to defeat him and regain the rule for 28 years.

He was fair and beneficent. He went to Turk's land to have revenge of his grandfather Iraj against Tur ibn Fereydun. It is said that his rule lasted for 120 years.

Kings of that time

One of the kings of that time was Arra'ish ibn Qais ibn Saifi ibn Saba ibn Yashgub ibn Ya'rub ibn Qahtan, he was one of the Yemeni kings after Ya'rub ibn Qhtan and his brothers. The kingdom of Yemen was during the rule of king Manuchehr. He conquered India and Turk. His son Abraha assumed the rule of his father who conquered the countries of Maghrib. Also, It was said that the kings of Yemen were employees for the Persian kings.

• CHAPTER 9 •

Tale of Moses (PBUH)

A There was 1000 years between Moses and Abraham and there were 1000 years between Abraham and Noah and between Noah and Adam.

He was Moses ibn Amram ibn Kehath ibn Levi ibn Jacob. His mother was Jochebed.

Pharaoh of Joseph was not hurting Banu Israel but he was very good to them, also, the pharaohs after him did not hurt them but the fourth pharaoh, Pharaoh of Moses, was the worst one of them, he lived for 300 years, he enslaved and tortured Banu Israel. He used them to work for him; some of them were builders, farmers and so on but the rest of them had to pay Jizyah.

Scholars said: Priests said to Pharaoh that there would be a baby who would be born in Banu Israel and destroy you". He ordered that all their children to be killed. Coptic complained that if he would continue doing that, there would not be people to serve them, then he ordered killing for a year and ceased it for the successive.

Aaron was born in the year that there was not any killing and Moses was born in the successive year. His mother feared to be killed, so she was inspired to cast him into the river and do not grieve. The water carried the wooden box of Moses and sent him to Pharaoh and the family of Pharaoh picked him up [out of the river]. Asiya, the wife of Pharaoh, said he was about more than a year old; he was born in this year. She said "He will be a comfort of the eye for me and for you. Do not kill him; perhaps he may benefit us, or we may adopt him as a son." Pharaoh did not have birth except for girls so he did not kill him.

The heart of Moses' mother became empty [of all else]. She was about to disclose [the matter concerning] him, had God not bound fast her heart. She was listening for news till she heard that Pharaoh took a boy in a wooden box, then she told his sister, Miriam: "Follow him"; so she watched him from a distance. She went to the house of Pharaoh and said: "Shall I direct you to a household that will be responsible for him for you while they are to him [for his upbringing] sincere?" they said who are they? She said the wife of Amram. Once, Pharaoh was carrying Moses, Moses hold his beard, Pharaoh became angry and decided to slaughter him but Asiya said that he was a boy and did not mind. She put a piece of lighted coal and corundum before Moses, Moses chose the piece of lighted coal and put it in his mouth that burnt his tongue, so Exalted is He says: "And untie the knot from my tongue"." "وَاحْلُلْ عُقْدَةً مِّن لِّسَانِي" (20:27).

Moses was riding ships of Pharaoh and wearing clothes like Pharaoh; He was called Moses son of Pharaoh. Once Moses had a ride in the city, he found two people fighting together, one of them from Banu Israel and the other from Coptic, the one from his faction asked his help against the enemy, so Moses struck him and killed him. Exalted is He says: "And he entered the city at a time of inattention by its people and found therein two men fighting: one from his faction and one from among his enemy. And the one from his faction called for help to him against the one from his enemy, so Moses struck him and [unintentionally] killed him"." "وَدَخَلَ الْمَدِينَةَ عَلَىٰ حِينِ غَفْلَةٍ مِّنْ أَهْلِهَا فَوَجَدَ فِيهَا رَجُلَيْنِ يَقْتَتِلَانِ هَٰذَا مِن شِيعَتِهِ وَهَٰذَا مِنْ عَدُوِّهِ فَاسْتَغَاثَهُ الَّذِي مِن شِيعَتِهِ عَلَى الَّذِي مِنْ عَدُوِّهِ فَوَكَزَهُ مُوسَىٰ فَقَضَىٰ عَلَيْهِ" (28:15). Moses repented on that and he became inside the city and anticipating exposure, "Suddenly the one who sought his help the previous day cried out to him [once again]"." فَإِذَا الَّذِي اسْتَنصَرَهُ بِالْأَمْسِ يَسْتَصْرِخُهُ" (28:18). Coptic had told Pharaoh about the killing, he said to them if you knew the killer, tell me. When Moses wanted to help the Israeli, he thought that Moses intended to hurt him, so he said: "O Moses, do you intend to kill me as you killed someone yesterday? You only want to be a tyrant in the land and do not want to be of the amenders"." "يَا مُوسَىٰ أَتُرِيدُ أَن تَقْتُلَنِي كَمَا قَتَلْتَ نَفْسًا بِالْأَمْسِ إِن تُرِيدُ إِلَّا أَن تَكُونَ جَبَّارًا فِي الْأَرْضِ وَمَا تُرِيدُ أَن تَكُونَ مِنَ الْمُصْلِحِينَ" (28:19).

People knew that Moses was the killer and wanted to seize him so he went out fearing, then God guided him to go to Midian. Exalted is He says: "And when he came to the well of Midian, he found there a crowd of people watering [their flocks], and he found aside from them two women driving back [their flocks]"." "وَلَمَّا وَرَدَ مَاءَ مَدْيَنَ وَجَدَ عَلَيْهِ أُمَّةً مِنَ النَّاسِ يَسْقُونَ وَوَجَدَ مِن دُونِهِمُ امْرَأَتَيْنِ تَذُودَانِ" (28:23). He asked them: "What is your circumstance?" They said, "We do not water until the shepherds dispatch [their flocks]; and our father is an old man"." "مَا خَطْبُكُمَا قَالَتَا لَا نَسْقِي حَتَّىٰ يُصْدِرَ الرِّعَاءُ وَأَبُونَا شَيْخٌ كَبِيرٌ" (28:23). Moses was merciful to them and moved the rock that blocks the well and helped them to water their flocks. Then he went back to the shade and said, "My Lord, indeed I am, for whatever good You would send down to me, in need"." "فَقَالَ رَبِّ إِنِّي لِمَا أَنزَلْتَ إِلَيَّ مِنْ خَيْرٍ فَقِيرٌ" (28:24). When the two girls went back to their father, he asked them and they told him the tale of Moses, He sent one of them To Moses asking him to come to see her father, Exalted is He says: "Then one of the two women came to him walking with shyness. She said, "Indeed, my father invites you that he may reward you for having watered for us.""." "فَجَاءَتْهُ إِحْدَاهُمَا تَمْشِي"

(28:25). "عَلَى اسْتِحْيَاءٍ قَالَتْ إِنَّ أَبِي يَدْعُوكَ لِيَجْزِيَكَ أَجْرَ مَا سَقَيْتَ لَنَا" He went with her to her father. When he reached her father, "So when he came to him and related to him the story"." فَلَمَّا جَاءَهُ وَقَصَّ عَلَيْهِ الْقَصَصَ" (28:25). One of them said: "O my father, hire him. Indeed, the best one you can hire is the strong and the trustworthy"." "يَا أَبَتِ اسْتَأْجِرْهُ إِنَّ خَيْرَ مَنِ اسْتَأْجَرْتَ الْقَوِيُّ الْأَمِينُ" (28:26). Her father said how did you know his honesty and strength, she said regarding his strength, he carries a stone that only more than ten men can carry it. Regarding his honesty, he said to her, 'walk behind me and describe the road to me' lest that the wind should blow and move your clothes then reveal your body'. When Shuaib heard her saying, he said: "Indeed, I wish to wed you one of these, my two daughters, on [the condition] that you serve me for eight years; but if you complete ten, it will be [as a favor] from you"." "إِنِّي أُرِيدُ أَنْ أُنكِحَكَ إِحْدَى ابْنَتَيَّ هَاتَيْنِ عَلَى أَن تَأْجُرَنِي ثَمَانِيَ حِجَجٍ فَإِنْ أَتْمَمْتَ عَشْرًا فَمِنْ عِندِكَ" (28:27). Then, Moses got married to the woman that called for him.

Exalted is He says: "When Moses had completed the term and was traveling with his family, he perceived from the direction of the mount a fire. He said to his family, "Stay here; indeed, I have perceived a fire'."." "فَلَمَّا قَضَىٰ مُوسَى الْأَجَلَ وَسَارَ بِأَهْلِهِ آنَسَ مِن جَانِبِ الطُّورِ نَارًا قَالَ لِأَهْلِهِ امْكُثُوا إِنِّي آنَسْتُ نَارًا" (28:29). When Moses saw the fire, he went till he became near to it, he found great fire in a very green tree, Moses did not know its tale standing in astonishment. He found that there was a great tree was fired but its great greenery hinders the fire. Then, he wanted to take a flame from it but he could not; he realized that that fire was for a matter. He confused about it, then he felt fear and sorrow.

While he was in that state he heard a voice calling him, Exalted is He says: "He was called from the right side of the valley in a blessed spot - from the tree, "O Moses, indeed I am God, Lord of the worlds"." "نُودِيَ مِن شَاطِئِ الْوَادِ الْأَيْمَنِ فِي الْبُقْعَةِ الْمُبَارَكَةِ مِنَ الشَّجَرَةِ أَن يَا مُوسَىٰ إِنِّي أَنَا اللَّـهُ رَبُّ الْعَالَمِينَ" (28:30). Moses asked his Lord: "Do I hear your messenger's voice or Yours?" God said: "I, who, talk to You, Moses." God asks him: "And what is that in your right hand, O Moses?"." "وَمَا تِلْكَ بِيَمِينِكَ يَا مُوسَىٰ" (20:17). Moses said, "It is my staff; I lean upon it, and I bring down leaves for my sheep and I have therein other uses"." "عَصَايَ أَتَوَكَّأُ عَلَيْهَا وَأَهُشُّ بِهَا عَلَىٰ غَنَمِي وَلِيَ فِيهَا مَآرِبُ أُخْرَىٰ" (20:18) God said to him: "Throw it down, O Moses"." "أَلْقِهَا يَا مُوسَىٰ" (20:19). He threw it down, and thereupon it was a snake, moving swiftly.

It was a great snake ever seen and when Moses saw it he felt great fear. Exalted is He says: "Seize it and fear not; We will return it to its former condition"." "خُذْهَا وَلَا تَخَفْ سَنُعِيدُهَا سِيرَتَهَا الْأُولَىٰ" (20:21). God said to Moses: "Come, be near do not afraid", till he rests his back against the tree and holds his stick. God said: "I give you a great position that is not enjoyed by anyone after you, go deliver my message; you are in Our eyes" Exalted is He says:

"Go to Pharaoh. Indeed, he has transgressed. And say to him, 'Would you [be willing to] purify yourself. And let me guide you to your Lord so you would fear [Him]?"

It is said that God told Moses to go to Pharaoh to deliver a message that "God left you 400 years during which you were challenging Him". Thus, God commanded Moses to go to him and stand against him, together with his brother Aaron. Exalted is He says: "Go to him and deliver my message to him and invite him to monotheism and worshipping Me". God said: "And do not extend your eyes toward that by which We have given enjoyment to [some] categories of them, [its being but] the splendor of worldly life."

Moses (PBUH) went to Pharaoh in his city, the city, that had four gates, he entered from the great gate so that Pharaoh could see him. When Moses entered to Pharaoh, he said to him: "Did we not raise you among us as a child, and you remained among us for years of your life?"" "أَلَمْ نُرَبِّكَ فِينَا وَلِيدًا وَلَبِثْتَ فِينَا مِنْ عُمُرِكَ سِنِينَ" (26:18). Moses delivered God's message, Pharaoh said: "Seize him." Then, "So [Moses] threw his staff, and suddenly it was a serpent manifest"." "فَأَلْقَىٰ عَصَاهُ فَإِذَا هِيَ ثُعْبَانٌ مُبِينٌ" (26:32). Pharaoh said to the close ones around him, "Indeed, this is a magician. He wants to drive you out of your land by his magic, so what do you advise?" They said, "Postpone [the matter of] him and his brother and send among the cities gatherers who will bring you every skilled magician."

Pharaoh said to Moses to decide a time to prove his message, forty days, but he refused. Then God revealed to him let them forty days. Some scholars said that the face of Moses becomes full of light for three days after talking to God.

Having spoken to God, Moses returned to his people and turned to Egypt till he reached it at night. Moses met his brother Aaron and they recognized each other and said to him that he had to go with him to Pharaoh. Moses and Aaron went to Pharaoh to deliver the message of God and let him see the great sign of the snake, but Pharaoh denied and disobeyed. Then he turned his back, striving, and he gathered [his people] and called out and said, "I am your most exalted lord." So the magicians were assembled for the reward day if they defeat Moses.

Regarding the number of magicians, it is controversial; some said they were 70000 magicians and some said they were 700000 magicians. They threw their ropes and their staffs and said, "By the might of Pharaoh, indeed it is we who are predominant." It was like that the valley was filled with heaps of snakes, Exalted is He says: "And he sensed within himself apprehension, did Moses. God said, "Fear not. Indeed, it is you who are superior"." "فَأَوْجَسَ فِي نَفْسِهِ خِيفَةً مُوسَىٰ. قُلْنَا لَا تَخَفْ إِنَّكَ أَنتَ الْأَعْلَىٰ" (20:67:68). God inspired him: "Throw what is in your right hand; it will swallow up what they have crafted. It is nothing, but the trick of a magician, and the magician will not succeed wherever he is." He obeyed and threw his stick that grabbed theirs. So the magicians fell down in prostration. They said, "We have believed in the Lord of Aaron and Moses." Pharaoh said, "You believed him before I gave you permission. Indeed, he is your leader who has taught you magic. So I will surely cut off your hands and your feet on opposite sides, and I will crucify you on the trunks of palm trees, and you will surely know which of us is more severe in [giving] punishment and more enduring." They said, "Never will we prefer you over what has come to us of clear proofs and [over] He who created us. Exalted is he says: "So decree whatever you are to decree. You can only decree for this worldly life"." "فاقض مَا أنتَ قَاضٍ. إنَّمَا تَقضِي هَذِهِ الحَيَاةَ الدُّنيَا" (20:72). He was defeated and ordered to kill the magicians.

Tale of signs that had occurred to Pharaoh's people.

When the tale of the magicians ended, the signs were sent to Pharaoh.

First: Flood: it was the rain that drowned everything. God sent upon them the flood, locusts, lice, frogs and blood as distinct signs, but they were arrogant and were criminals. When the punishment descended upon them, they said, "O Moses, invoke for us your Lord by what He has promised you. If you [can] remove the punishment, we will surely believe you, and we will send with you the Children of Israel."

Ibn Abbas said that Moses spent 20 years after the tale of the magicians inviting people of Pharaoh. Scholars said that God revealed to Moses saying: "And speak to him with gentle speech that perhaps he may be reminded or fear [God]"." فقولا له "قَوْلًا لَيِّنًا لَعَلَّهُ يَتَذَكَّرُ أَوْ يَخْشَىٰ" (20:44). They said, "Our Lord, indeed we are afraid that he will hasten [punishment] against us or that he will transgress." God said to them: "So go to him and say, 'Indeed, we are messengers of your Lord, so send with us the Children of Israel and do not torment them. We have come to you with a sign from your Lord. And peace will be upon he who follows the guidance." Pharaoh said: "I am your most exalted lord"." "أَنَا رَبُّكُمُ الْأَعْلَىٰ" (79:24). "O eminent ones, I have not known you to have a god other than me. Then ignite for me, O Haman, [a fire] upon the clay and make for me a tower that I may look at the God of Moses. And indeed, I do think he is among the liars." "وَقَالَ فِرْعَوْنُ يَا أَيُّهَا الْمَلَأُ مَا عَلِمْتُ لَكُم مِّنْ إِلَٰهٍ غَيْرِي فَأَوْقِدْ لِي يَا هَامَانُ عَلَى الطِّينِ فَاجْعَل لِّي صَرْحًا لَّعَلِّي أَطَّلِعُ إِلَىٰ إِلَٰهِ مُوسَىٰ وَإِنِّي لَأَظُنُّهُ مِنَ الْكَاذِبِينَ" (28:38) His people said to Pharaoh: "Will you leave Moses and his people to cause corruption in the land and abandon you and your gods?"." أَتَذَرُ "مُوسَىٰ وَقَوْمَهُ لِيُفْسِدُوا فِي الْأَرْضِ وَيَذَرَكَ وَآلِهَتَكَ" (7:127). [Pharaoh] said,

"We will kill their sons and keep their women alive; and indeed, we are subjugators over them."

Tale of a believer to Moses from the family of Pharaoh

A believing man from the family of Pharaoh who concealed his faith said, "Do you kill a man [merely] because he says, 'My Lord is God'"." "أَتَقْتُلُونَ رَجُلًا أَنْ يَقُولَ رَبِّيَ اللهُ" (40:28). He was always defending Moses, avoiding him killing. He argues that Moses had brought Pharaoh clear proofs from his Lord? And if he should have been lying, then upon him would be [the consequence of] his lie; but if he should have been truthful, he would strike Pharaoh some of what he promised. Indeed, God does not guide one who is a transgressor and a liar. Some said he was called Simeon, Shamoun or Samaan.

Asiya is one from those who believed in Moses

Pharaoh made strings in the legs and arms of his wife Asiya and when they leave her the angels covered her, She said: "My Lord, build for me near You a house in Heaven and save me from Pharaoh and his deeds and save me from the wrongdoing people"." "رَبِّ ابْنِ لِي عِندَكَ بَيْتًا فِي الْجَنَّةِ وَنَجِّنِي مِن فِرْعَوْنَ وَعَمَلِهِ وَنَجِّنِي مِنَ الْقَوْمِ".

"الظَّالِمِينَ" (66:11). God disclosed her house in the Heaven before her death.

Abu Musa narrated that Prophet Mohammed (PBUH) said: "the best women in the Heaven are Khadijah bint Khuwaylid, Fatima bint Mohammed, Miriam and Asiya the wife of Pharaoh."

Also, from those who believed in Moses is the woman who combed the hair of Pharaoh's daughter (Hairdresser).

It was narrated by Ubayy ibn Kaab that on the night when the Messenger of God (PBUH) was taken on the Night Journey (Isra'), he (PBUH) noticed a good fragrance and said: "O Gabriel, what is this good fragrance?" He said: "This is the fragrance of the grave of the hairdresser, her two sons and husband." While she was combing the hair of Pharaoh's daughter, she dropped the comb and said: 'May Pharaoh perish!' (The daughter) told her father about that. The woman had two sons and a husband. (Pharaoh) sent for them, and tried to make the woman and her husband give up their religion, but they refused. He said: 'I am going to kill you.' They said: 'It would be an act of kindness on your part, if you kill us, to put us in one grave.' So he did that." Pharaoh ordered a great brass pot to be fired under it till it was very hot and he took her children and ordered to be thrown before her one by one in the pot then he put her at the end.

Tale of the drowning

Exalted is he says: "And We had inspired to Moses, "Travel by night with My servants and strike for them a dry path through the sea; you will not fear being overtaken [by Pharaoh] nor be afraid [of drowning]"." وَلَقَدْ أَوْحَيْنَا إِلَىٰ مُوسَىٰ أَنْ أَسْرِ بِعِبَادِي فَاضْرِبْ لَهُمْ طَرِيقًا "فِي الْبَحْرِ يَبَسًا لَا تَخَافُ دَرَكًا وَلَا تَخْشَىٰ" (20:77). Moses commanded Banu Israel to borrow jewelry from Coptic and they went out at night. They were 620000 persons. Moses went out with the coffin of Joseph (PBUH) to bury him beside his fathers in the sacred land.

When Joseph (PBUH) was about to die, He asked Banu Israel and swore by God not to get out from Egypt except after getting his bones with them. Moses was 80 years old when he was about to get out of Egypt. It is said that there were 505 years between the birth of Abraham and Moses' getting out from Egypt and there were 3840 years between landing of Adam and the getting out of Moses from Egypt.

Moses invoked his Lord: "Our Lord, indeed You have given Pharaoh and his establishment splendor and wealth in the worldly life, our Lord, that they may lead [men] astray from Your way. Our Lord, obliterate their wealth and harden their hearts so that they will not believe until they see the painful punishment"." "رَبَّنَا إِنَّكَ آتَيْتَ فِرْعَوْنَ وَمَلَأَهُ زِينَةً وَأَمْوَالًا فِي الْحَيَاةِ الدُّنْيَا رَبَّنَا لِيُضِلُّوا عَن سَبِيلِكَ رَبَّنَا اطْمِسْ عَلَىٰ أَمْوَالِهِمْ وَاشْدُدْ عَلَىٰ قُلُوبِهِمْ فَلَا يُؤْمِنُوا حَتَّىٰ يَرَوُا الْعَذَابَ الْأَلِيمَ" (10:88).

They went out at night; Pharaoh followed them with an army of 1600000 knights headed by Hamman. "When the two companies saw one another, the companions of Moses said, "Indeed, we are to be overtaken!"." "فَلَمَّا تَرَاءَى الْجَمْعَانِ قَالَ أَصْحَابُ مُوسَىٰ إِنَّا لَمُدْرَكُونَ" (26:61). They said that the sea was before them and Pharaoh and his soldiers were behind them. Moses said, "No! Indeed, with me is my Lord; He will guide me"." "كَلَّا إِنَّ مَعِيَ رَبِّي سَيَهْدِينِ" (26:62).

God inspired to Moses, "Strike with your staff the sea," and it parted, and each portion was like a great towering mountain. Moses and his people walked through on a land while there were two walls of water on both sides. Pharaoh and his soldiers followed Moses and while they were all got in the sea, the two walls of water fell upon them, drowning all of them. Exalted is He says: "And We took the Children of Israel across the sea, and Pharaoh and his soldiers pursued them in tyranny and enmity until, when drowning overtook him, he said, "I believe that there is no deity except that in whom the Children of Israel believe, and I am of the Muslims"." وَجَاوَزْنَا بِبَنِي إِسْرَائِيلَ الْبَحْرَ فَأَتْبَعَهُمْ فِرْعَوْنُ وَجُنُودُهُ بَغْيًا وَعَدْوًا حَتَّىٰ إِذَا أَدْرَكَهُ الْغَرَقُ قَالَ آمَنتُ أَنَّهُ لَا إِلَٰهَ إِلَّا الَّذِي آمَنَتْ بِهِ بَنُو إِسْرَائِيلَ وَأَنَا مِنَ الْمُسْلِمِينَ" (10:90).

Ibn Abbas narrated that the Messenger of God (PBUH) said: "When God drowned Pharaoh he said: 'I believe that there is no god except the One that the children of Israel believe in.' So Gabriel said: 'O Muhammad! If you could only have seen me, while I was taking (the mud) from the sea, and filling his mouth out of fear that the mercy would reach him.'"

Some scholars said that Pharaoh was not drowned and the sea threw him on the beach, Exalted is He says: "So today We will save you in body that you may be to those who succeed you a sign. And indeed, many among the people, of Our signs, are heedless"." فَالْيَوْمَ نُنَجِّيكَ بِبَدَنِكَ لِتَكُونَ لِمَنْ خَلْفَكَ آيَةً وَإِنَّ كَثِيرًا مِّنَ النَّاسِ عَنْ آيَاتِنَا لَغَافِلُونَ" (10:92).

It was narrated by ibn Abbas that the companions of Moses who passed the sea were 12 tribes, they were all from the children of Jacob (PBUH).

One of the events:
    Banu Israel asked Moses to make for them a god

Exalted is He says: "And We took the Children of Israel across the sea; then they came upon a people intent in devotion to [some] idols of theirs. They said, "O Moses, make for us a god just as they have gods." He said, "Indeed, you are a people behaving ignorantly"." وَجَاوَزْنَا بِبَنِي إِسْرَائِيلَ الْبَحْرَ فَأَتَوْا عَلَىٰ قَوْمٍ يَعْكُفُونَ عَلَىٰ أَصْنَامٍ لَهُمْ قَالُوا يَا مُوسَى اجْعَل لَّنَا إِلَٰهًا كَمَا لَهُمْ آلِهَةٌ قَالَ إِنَّكُمْ قَوْمٌ تَجْهَلُونَ" (7:138). Indeed, those [worshippers] - destroyed is that in which they are [engaged], and worthless is whatever they were doing. Moses said, "Is it other than God I should desire for you as a god while He has preferred you over the worlds?"

Tale of their request for forgiveness

When they became sorrowful, they asked for acceptance of their repentance, Exalted is He says: "And [recall] when Moses said to his people, "O my people, indeed you have wronged yourselves by your taking of the calf [for worship]. So repent to your Creator and kill yourselves. That is best for [all of] you in the sight of your Creator." Then He accepted your repentance; indeed, He is the Accepting of repentance, the Merciful"." وَإِذْ قَالَ مُوسَىٰ لِقَوْمِهِ يَا قَوْمِ إِنَّكُمْ ظَلَمْتُمْ أَنفُسَكُم بِاتِّخَاذِكُمُ الْعِجْلَ فَتُوبُوا إِلَىٰ بَارِئِكُمْ فَاقْتُلُوا أَنفُسَكُمْ ذَٰلِكُمْ خَيْرٌ لَّكُمْ عِندَ بَارِئِكُمْ فَتَابَ عَلَيْكُمْ إِنَّهُ هُوَ التَّوَّابُ الرَّحِيمُ" (2:54).

Scholars said that when they commanded to kill themselves, they said how we can kill our children. God afflicted them with darkness not see each other. They continued to kill themselves till Moses asked God Exalted to forgive them.

History of Natioans (1)

There was the event of when Moses took his companions and went to Mount Sinai to give excuses for having a calf for worship. Moses asked 70 men of them to go out to the mount to ask for forgiveness and repent for their people.

When they reached the mount they said to Moses: "O Moses, we will never believe you until we see God outright"; so the thunderbolt took you while you were looking on"." "يَا مُوسَىٰ لَن نُّؤْمِنَ لَكَ حَتَّىٰ نَرَى اللَّـهَ جَهْرَةً فَأَخَذَتْكُمُ الصَّاعِقَةُ وَأَنتُمْ تَنظُرُونَ" (2:55). Moses said: "My Lord, if You had willed, You could have destroyed them before and me [as well]"." "لَوْ شِئْتَ أَهْلَكْتَهُم مِّن قَبْلُ وَإِيَّايَ" (7:155). Then God revived them after their death that perhaps they would be grateful.

Tale of Jericho

God, Exalted is He, inspired to Moses and his people to go to Jericho, it is a place in Jerusalem. Scholars said that when they were about it, Moses sent twelve men from all the tribes of Banu Israel to collect information about people of tyrannies. They were seized by one of them who decided to set them free to tell their people about what they saw. The twelve men decided not to tell their people about that except Moses but ten of them told their people about what happened to them, people said to Moses: "O Moses, indeed within it is a people of tyrannical strength,

and indeed, we will never enter it until they leave it"." يَا مُوسَىٰ إِنَّ
 "فِيهَا قَوْمًا جَبَّارِينَ وَإِنَّا لَن نَّدْخُلَهَا حَتَّىٰ يَخْرُجُوا مِنْهَا" (5:22). They said, "O Moses, indeed we will not enter it, ever, as long as they are within it; so go, you and your Lord, and fight. Indeed, we are remaining right here." Moses said, "O' my Lord, indeed I do not possess except myself and my brother, so part us from the defiantly disobedient people." God said, "Then indeed, it is forbidden to them for forty years [in which] they will wander throughout the land. So do not grieve over the defiantly disobedient people."

Event of the stone

When they went out of the sea, they needed water, Moses asked God to send them water. God revealed: "Strike with your staff the stone". Therefore, there gushed forth from it twelve springs.

Event of revealing Torah

They asked Moses to get them a book from God; God made an appointment with Moses for thirty nights and perfected them by [the addition of] ten; so the term of his Lord was completed as forty nights and gave him Torah and had revealed to him 10 scriptures, too. God imposed two prayers every day and Hajj.

Also, the event of raising the mountain above them

God raised the mountain above them as if it was a dark cloud and they were certain that it would fall upon them, God said: "Take what We have given you with determination and remember what is in it that you might fear God." This event was happened when they were given Torah and after they had asked for it, but they found it difficult to follow.

Also, the event of Calf's tale
Gabriel came to Moses to take him to talk with his Lord.

Moses set off and appointed his brother Aaron to be after him and promised them that he was going to talk with God for thirty nights and perfected them by [the addition of] ten by God, Exalted is He. During this additional period, they worshiped the Calf. The Samiri came to them with a calf from their ornaments – an image having a lowing sound. The Samiri was one of the people who worshipped the cows so his heart was full of this worship. Exalted is He says: "And he extracted for them [the statue of] a calf which had a lowing sound, and they said, "This is your god and the god of Moses, but he forgot"." فَأَخْرَجَ لَهُمْ عِجْلًا جَسَدًا لَهُ خُوَارٌ فقالُوا هَٰذَا إِلَٰهُكُمْ وَإِلَٰهُ مُوسَىٰ فَنَسِيَ " (20:88). He said to them that Moses left his God and went to search for him, so they continued to worship it, Aaron had already told them before [the return of Moses], "O my people, you are only being tested by it, and indeed, your Lord is the Most Merciful, so follow me and obey my order."

Exalted is He told Moses about this story: "But indeed, We have tried your people after you [departed], and the Samiri has led them astray"." "فَإِنَّا قَدْ فَتَنَّا قَوْمَكَ مِن بَعْدِكَ وَأَضَلَّهُمُ السَّامِرِيُّ" (20:85).

Moses asked God to see him: "My Lord, show me [Yourself] that I may look at You." [God] said, "You will not see Me, but look at the mountain; if it should remain in place, then you will see Me." But when his Lord appeared to the mountain, He rendered it level, and Moses fell unconscious. And when he awoke, he said, "Exalted are You! I have repented to You, and I am the first of the believers"." رَبِّ أَرِنِي أَنظُرْ إِلَيْكَ قَالَ لَن تَرَانِي وَلَٰكِنِ انظُرْ إِلَى الْجَبَلِ فَإِنِ اسْتَقَرَّ مَكَانَهُ فَسَوْفَ تَرَانِي فَلَمَّا تَجَلَّىٰ رَبُّهُ لِلْجَبَلِ جَعَلَهُ دَكًّا وَخَرَّ مُوسَىٰ صَعِقًا فَلَمَّا أَفَاقَ قَالَ سُبْحَانَكَ تُبْتُ إِلَيْكَ وَأَنَا أَوَّلُ الْمُؤْمِنِينَ" (7:143).

Moses took the Tablets of the Stone and returned to his people, angry and grieved, he said, "How wretched is that by which you have replaced me after [my departure]. Were you impatient over the matter of your Lord?" And he threw down the tablets and seized his brother by [the hair of] his head, pulling him toward him. [Aaron] said, "O son of my mother, indeed the people oppressed me and were about to kill me, so let not the enemies rejoice over me and do not place me among the wrongdoing people."

Moses said: "And what is your case, O Samiri?"." فَمَا خَطْبُكَ يَا سَامِرِيُّ" (20:95). He said, "I saw what they did not see, so I took a handful [of dust] from the track of the messenger and threw it, and thus did my soul entice me"." بَصُرْتُ بِمَا لَمْ يَبْصُرُوا بِهِ فَقَبَضْتُ قَبْضَةً مِّنْ أَثَرِ الرَّسُولِ فَنَبَذْتُهَا وَكَذَلِكَ سَوَّلَتْ لِي نَفْسِي" (20:96). Moses said: "Look at your 'god' to which you remained devoted. We will surely burn it and blow it into the sea with a blast".

From these events, Said two men from those who feared [to disobey] upon whom God had bestowed favor, "Enter upon them through the gate, for when you have entered it, you will be predominant. And upon God rely, if you should be believers." They said, "O Moses, indeed we will not enter it, ever, as long as they are within it"." إِنَّا لَن نَّدْخُلَهَا أَبَدًا مَّا دَامُوا فِيهَا" (5:24). Moses said, "My Lord, indeed I do not possess except myself and my brother, so part us from the defiantly disobedient people"." رَبِّ إِنِّي لَا أَمْلِكُ إِلَّا نَفْسِي وَأَخِي فَافْرُقْ بَيْنَنَا وَبَيْنَ الْقَوْمِ الْفَاسِقِينَ" (5:25). God said: "Then indeed, it is forbidden to them for forty years [in which] they will wander throughout the land"." فَإِنَّهَا مُحَرَّمَةٌ عَلَيْهِمْ أَرْبَعِينَ سَنَةً يَتِيهُونَ فِي الْأَرْضِ" (5:26).

When they were punished with being wanderers, Moses became sorrowful for them. They said how we could eat. God sent down upon them manna and quails. They asked him for water, Moses stroke with his staff the stone, and there gushed forth from it twelve springs; each tribe drank from a spring. They asked Moses the shade, they were shaded with clouds. Then, they said: "O Moses, we can never endure one [kind of] food. So call upon your Lord to bring forth for us from the earth its green herbs and its cucumbers and its garlic and its lentils and its onions"." "لن نَصْبِرَ عَلَىٰ طَعَامٍ وَاحِدٍ فَادْعُ لَنَا رَبَّكَ يُخْرِجْ لَنَا مِمَّا تُنبِتُ الْأَرْضُ مِن بَقْلِهَا وَقِثَّائِهَا وَفُومِهَا وَعَدَسِهَا وَبَصَلِهَا" (2:61). When they went out from the land of wandering, they ate the grains.

Tale of Khadir (PBUH)

Some of scholars said that Khadir was in a time before Moses; some said he was the king Fereydun who defeated king Zahak. Some said he was in the time of Dhulqarnayn. Some said he was a child of those who believed in Abraham; there were many sayings about him.

Name of Khadir

History of Natioans (1)

Some people of the Book said: He was Khadirun ibn 'Amil ibn Alifrin ibn Esua ibn Isaac, the son of Dhulqarnayn's aunt and his minister. It is said that he was the fourth son of Adam.

Scholars said he was so-named as he sat on dry land, it became green with plants. There were many narrations about why he was called Khadir.

Tale of meeting of Moses with Khadir (PBUH)

It was narrated that the Prophet (PBUH) said: "Moses (PBUH) stood up to give sermon to the people of Israel. He was asked as to who amongst the people has the best knowledge, whereupon he said: I have the best knowledge." Thereupon God was annoyed with him that he did not attribute (the best knowledge) to Him. He inspired him: "A servant amongst My servants is at the junction of two rivers who has more knowledge than yours." Moses said: How can I meet him? It was said to him: "Carry a fish in the large basket and the place where you find it missing there you will find him." Thereupon, Moses proceeded forth along with a young man (Yusha'). Joshua b. Nan and Moses (PBUH) put the fish in the basket and there went along with him the young man (Yusha') until they came to a certain rock and Moses and his companion went to sleep and the fish stirred in that basket and fell into the ocean and God stopped the current of water like a vault until the way was made for the fish. Moses and his young companion were astonished and they walked for the rest of the day and the night and the friend of Moses forgot to inform him of this incident. When it was morning, Moses (PBUH) said to the young man: "Bring us our morning meal. We have certainly suffered in this, our journey, [much] fatigue"." (18:63). "آتِنَا غَدَاءَنَا لَقَدْ لَقِينَا مِنْ سَفَرِنَا هَٰذَا نَصَبًا". They did not feel exhausted until they had passed that place where they had been commanded (to stay). He said: "Did you see when we retired to the rock? Indeed, I forgot [there] the fish. And none made me forget it except Satan - that I should mention it. And it took its course into the sea amazingly"." أَرَأَيْتَ إِذْ أَوَيْنَا إِلَى "الصَّخْرَةِ فَإِنِّي نَسِيتُ الْحُوتَ وَمَا أَنْسَانِيهُ إِلَّا الشَّيْطَانُ أَنْ أَذْكُرَهُ وَاتَّخَذَ سَبِيلَهُ فِي الْبَحْرِ عَجَبًا" (18:63). Moses said: "That is what we were seeking." So they returned, following their footprints"." ذَٰلِكَ مَا كُنَّا نَبْغِ فَارْتَدَّا عَلَىٰ آثَارِهِمَا "قَصَصًا" (18:64). Then both of them retraced their steps until they reached Sakhra; there they saw a man covered with a cloth. Moses greeted him with peace. Khadir said to him: Where is peace in our country? He said: I am Moses, whereupon he (Khadir) said: You mean the Moses of Banu Israel? He said: Yes. Moses (PBUH) said to him: "May I follow you on [the condition] that you teach me from what you have been taught of sound judgment?"." (18:66). "هَلْ أَتَّبِعُكَ عَلَىٰ أَنْ تُعَلِّمَنِ مِمَّا عُلِّمْتَ رُشْدًا" He said: "Indeed, with me you will never be able to have patience"." إِنَّكَ لَن تَسْتَطِيعَ مَعِيَ صَبْرًا" (18:67). He (Khadir) said: You have knowledge out of the knowledge of God which in fact God imparted to you and about that I know nothing and I have knowledge out of God's knowledge which He imparted to me and about that you know nothing. How you will be able to bear that about which you do not know? Moses said: "You will find me, if God wills, patient, and I will not disobey you in [any] order "." سَتَجِدُنِي إِن شَاءَ اللَّـهُ صَابِرًا وَلَا أَعْصِي لَكَ أَمْرًا" (18:69).

Khadir said to him: If you were to follow me, then do not ask me about anything until I myself speak about it. He said: 'Yes'. So Khadir and Moses set forth on the bank of the river that there came before them a boat. Both of them talked to the owners of the boat, so that they might carry both of them. They had recognized Khadir and they carried them. Khadir thereupon took hold of a plank in the boat and broke it away. Moses said: These people have carried us without any charge and you attempt to break their boat so that the people sailing in the boat may drown. This is (something) grievous that you have done. He said: "Did I not say that with me you would never be able to have patience?"." أَلَمْ أَقُلْ إِنَّكَ لَن تَسْتَطِيعَ مَعِيَ صَبْرًا" (18:72). Moses said: "Do not blame me for what I forgot and do not cover me in my matter with difficult "." لَا تُؤَاخِذْنِي بِمَا نَسِيتُ وَلَا تُرْهِقْنِي مِنْ أَمْرِي عُسْرًا" (18:73). It was the first time Moses forgot.

Then both of them got down from the boat and began to walk along the coastline that they saw a boy who had been playing with other boys. Khadir pulled up his head and killed him. Moses said: "Have you killed a pure soul for other than [having killed] a soul? You have certainly done a deplorable thing"." قَتَلْتَ "نَفْسًا زَكِيَّةً بِغَيْرِ نَفْسٍ لَقَدْ جِئْتَ شَيْئًا نُكْرًا" (18:74). Thereupon he said: "Did I not say that with me you would never be able to have patience?"." "أَلَمْ أَقُلْ إِنَّكَ لَن تَسْتَطِيعَ مَعِيَ صَبْرًا" (18:72). He (Moses) further said: "If I ask you about anything after this, keep not company with me, then you would no doubt find (a plausible) excuse for this."

Exalted is He says: "So they set out, until when they came to the people of a town, they asked its people for food, but they refused to offer them hospitality. And they found therein a wall about to collapse, so al-Khidher restored it. [Moses] said, "If you wished, you could have taken for it a payment"." انطَلَقَا حَتَّى إِذَا أَتَيَا أَهْلَ قَرْيَةٍ اسْتَطْعَمَا أَهْلَهَا فَأَبَوْا أَن يُضَيِّفُوهُمَا فَوَجَدَا فِيهَا جِدَارًا يُرِيدُ أَن يَنقَضَّ فَأَقَامَهُ قَالَ لَوْ شِئْتَ لَاتَّخَذْتَ عَلَيْهِ أَجْرًا" (18:77). He (Khadir) said: "This is parting between me and you"." "هَذَا فِرَاقُ بَيْنِي وَبَيْنِكَ" (18:78).

Scholars differed regarding the life and death of Khadir.

Some scholars argued that he was still alive. There are Hadiths regarding Khadir. Some Hadiths narrate that Khadir lived during Dhulqarnayn and he drank from the spring which gave him eternal life. Those Hadiths are nullified as Exalted is He says to the Prophet (PBUH): "And We did not grant to any man before you eternity [on earth]; so if you die - would they be eternal?"."وَمَا جَعَلْنَا لِبَشَرٍ مِّن قَبْلِكَ الْخُلْدَ أَفَإِن مِّتَّ فَهُمُ الْخَالِدُونَ" (21:34). It is only Iblis who has bestowed eternal life, Exalted is He says: "So indeed, you are of those reprieved until the Day of the time well-known"."قَالَ فَإِنَّكَ مِنَ الْمُنظَرِينَ إِلَىٰ يَوْمِ الْوَقْتِ الْمَعْلُومِ" (15:37-38).

Tale of Korah (Qarun)

It is said: Qarun is the cousin of Moses; He is Qarun ibn Yashur ibn Kohath, Moses is ibn Amram ibn Kohath.

Qarun was from the people of Moses, but he tyrannized them. And God gave him of treasures whose keys would burden a band of strong men. Thereupon, his people said to him, "Do not exult. Indeed, God does not like the exultant. But seek, through that which God has given you, the home of the Hereafter; and [yet], do not forget your share of the world. And do good as God has done good to you. And desire not corruption in the land. Indeed, God does not like corrupters." He said: "I was only given it because of knowledge I have"."إِنَّمَا أُوتِيتُهُ عَلَىٰ عِلْمٍ عِندِي" (28:78). Exalted is He says: "Did he not know that God had destroyed before him of generations those who were greater than

him in power and greater in accumulation [of wealth]?"." أَوَلَمْ يَعْلَمْ
"أَنَّ اللَّـهَ قَدْ أَهْلَكَ مِن قَبْلِهِ مِنَ الْقُرُونِ مَنْ هُوَ أَشَدُّ مِنْهُ قُوَّةً وَأَكْثَرُ جَمْعًا" (28:78).

His people advised him but he intensified his tyranny. He came out before his people in his adornment. God caused the earth to swallow him and his home. And there was for him no company to aid him other than God, nor was he of those who [could] defend themselves. It is said that when Zakah was revealed to Moses, Qarun went to account what he had to pay, he found it very much. Then, he gathered his people and said: "Moses came to take your properties", they said to him "you were the greatest one of us, command us". He said to them that they would give money for adultery woman so that she could pretend that Moses did the sin of adultery with her.

They went to Moses saying that he committed adultery with a woman from Banu Israel. He said: 'Call her' when she came he said to her: "did I do?" She replied that they told lies as they offered her money to say that he did. Moses prostrated to his God, God inspired him that he could ask earth to do whatever he wanted, so he said to it to take them all. Earth did.

Tale of Banu Israel when they ascribed to Moses having scrotal hernia

History of Natioans (1)

Some of Banu Israel said that nothing prevents Moses from taking a bath with us except that he has a scrotal hernia as he used to take bath alone.

Abu Huraira narrated that the Prophet (PBUH) said, 'The (people of) Banu Israel used to take bath naked (all together) looking at each other. The Prophet (PBUH) Moses used to take a bath alone. They said, 'By God! Nothing prevents Moses from taking a bath with us except that he has a scrotal hernia.' So once Moses went out to take a bath and put his clothes over a stone and then that stone ran away with his clothes. Moses followed that stone saying, "My clothes, O' stone! My clothes, O stone! till the people of Banu Israel saw him and said, 'By God, Moses has got no defect in his body. Moses took his clothes and began to beat the stone." Abu Huraira added, "By God! There are still six or seven marks present on the stone from that excessive beating."

Tale of Kings during the time of Moses

It is said that the first king of Yemen during the time of Moses was from Himyar, who was called: Shumair ibn Alahlook, who built Zafar in Yemen and fired Amalek from it; he was from the employees of the Persian's kings on Yemen.

Aaron death is one of the events that occurred in the Time of Moses (PBUH)

It is said that God revealed to Moses that Aaron is going to be died and told him (Moses) to take his brother to a certain place to die there, He did. When Moses returned to his people and told them that Aaron died, they said that Moses killed his brother because of being loved by Banu Israel. Moses complained to God, God revealed to him to take them to his grave and He will give him life again to say to them the truth.

Scholars said that Aaron died before Moses during being wanderers and Moses buried him in a cave. When he went back to Banu Israel, they said that Moses killed his brother envying him on the love of Banu Israel. He complained to His God. God revealed to Moses to go to the grave. Moses took them and went to the grave and called his brother 'O' Aaron' Aaron replied and told them about his death.

Scholars said that Aaron died when he was 118 years old 3 years before the death of Moses. In Torah, he died when he was 120 years old during the time of being wanderers.

Death of Moses

There are many narrations about the death of Moses (PBUH) but the most correct one is that which was narrated by Abu Huraira that the Angel of Death was sent to Moses (PBUH) to inform him of his Lord's summons. When he came, he (Moses) boxed him and his eye was knocked out. He (the Angel of Death) came back to the Lord and said: You sent me to a servant, who did not want to die. God restored his eye to its proper place (and revived his eyesight), and then said: Go back to him and tell him that if he wants life he must place his hand on the back of an ox, and he would be granted as many years of life as the number of hairs covered by his hand. The Angel of Death returned to Moses informing him of this, he said: "and what would happen" then the Angel replied: "Then you must court death". Moses said: So, let it be now, not later". And he supplicated God to bring him close to the sacred land. Thereupon, God's Messenger (PBUH) said: "If I were there, I would have shown you his grave beside the road at the red mound."

Scholars said that Moses died three years after Aaron. It is said that Moses died when he was 120 years old; 20 years was during the time of king Fereydun and 100 years was during Manuchehr. The time of his prophecy was during king Manuchehr. Scholars differed regarding whether Moses died in the Levant or no; some said he and his brother died during being wanderers. There is another opinion which is the most correct one: Moses and his people lived wanderers for 40 years, and then they entered the village where he said to them enter the village and eat whatever you want. Scholars said that Moses is the one who conquered the village of people of tyrannical strength and he is the killer of Og, their king.

Scholars said that Jews do not know where the graves of Aaron and Moses, if they knew, they would worship them as gods.

• CHAPTER 10 •

Tale of Joshua ibn Nun (PBUH)

He is Joshua ibn Nun ibn Ephraim ibn Joseph ibn Jacob

It is said that God, Exalted is He, made Joshua a prophet during the time of Moses; God sent him to Banu Israel to execute the provisions of Torah; who divided the Levant among Banu Israel's tribes. He is the one that God created Jordon River for him; God commanded him to march to Jericho to fight against people of tyrannical strength. Joshua entered Jericho with the Israelis where he fought the people of the tyrannical strength with the help of God, there Joshua asked them to give pledge to him.

Abu Huraira narrated that the Prophet (PBUH) said, "A prophet amongst the prophets carried out a holy military expedition, so he said to his followers, 'Anyone who has married a woman and wants to consummate the marriage, and has not done so yet, should not accompany me; nor should a man who has built a house but has not completed its roof; nor a man who has sheep or she camels and is waiting for the birth of their young ones.' So, the prophet carried out the expedition and when he reached that town at the time or nearly at the time of the `Asr prayer.

He said to the sun, 'O sun! You are under God's Order and I am under God's Order. O' God! Stop it (i.e. the sun) from setting.' It was stopped till God made him victorious. Then he collected the booty and the fire came to burn it, but it was not burned. He said (to his men), 'Some of you have stolen something from the booty.

So one man from every tribe should give me a pledge of allegiance by shaking hands with me.' (They did so and) the hand of a man got stuck over the hand of their prophet. Then that prophet said (to the man), 'The theft has been committed by your people. So all the persons of your tribe should give me the pledge of allegiance by shaking hands with me.' The hands of two or three men got stuck over the hand of their prophet and he said, "You have committed the theft.' Then they brought a head of gold like the head of a cow and put it there, and the fire came and consumed the booty. The Prophet (PBUH) added: Then God saw our weakness and disability, so he made booty legal for us."

History of Natioans (1)

It is said that God revealed to Joshua (PBUH) that God would cause death for 40000 from the good people and 60000 from the evil people of his people. He said what about the good people?! God said that they did not be angry for sake of Him and they were eating and drinking with them.

Joshua continued to conquer all Amalek kings till he killed about 31 kings of them and divided all the lands which he conquered.

Joshua (PBUH) died while he was 110 years old and some said 120 years old, he was buried in Mount Ephraim. He was managing the affairs of Banu Israel for 27 years till he died and after the death of Moses; there was 20 years during the rule of king Manuchehr and 7 years during the rule of king Afrasiab.

Tale of events that happened after Joshua (PBUH)

When Joshua was about to die, he appointed Caleb ibn Jephunneh, he was not a prophet but a righteous man who became their leader guiding them to worship God, like Joshua did till his death.

Caleb appointed his son as a leader for them who ruled Banu Israel in justice for forty years. When he died Banu Israel's tribes disagreed and divided into tribes, then they committed sins and loved the kingship.

Tale of kings after Joshua (PBUH)

King Manuchehr died during the time of Joshua, then, Afrasiab became the king. There were many kings after them who were very tyrannical. Then, there was one of the children of Manuchehr who expelled them from the kingdom and reclaimed the land. He ruled for three years. His son, Keyqubad, assumed the rule. He fought Turks for years preventing them to violate the borders of the Persian Kingdom. His rule was for 100 years; during this time, there were Joshua, Caleb ibn Jephunneh then Hazel.

Tale of Hazel ibn Buzi

It is said that he was the man who supplicated to God regarding: "Those who left their homes in many thousands, fearing death?"."الَّذِينَ خَرَجُوا مِن دِيَارِهِمْ وَهُمْ أُلُوفٌ حَذَرَ الْمَوْتِ" (2:243).

It is said that there were people from Banu Israel was afflicted with a disaster; they complained saying they wished that they would die. God inspired Hazel to say to them that there was no rest by death. God said to him to go to a place where there were 4000 dead people; it is said that they were the people where God says: "Those who left their homes in many thousands, fearing death?"." "الَّذِينَ خَرَجُوا مِن دِيَارِهِمْ وَهُمْ أُلُوفٌ حَذَرَ الْمَوْتِ" (2:243). God asked Hazel if he wanted to see how God grant life for the dead. Hazel said 'Yes'. God said to him to call for them, they returned to life. Many narrations were reported about this story.

Tale of Kings during Hazel

There was Nebuchadnezzar; who killed the kings of that time and there were many prophets like Jeremiah and Daniel. When Hazel died, there were many events that happened to them, so God sent them Elias; some said that Hazel is after Elias.

CHAPTER 11

Tale of Elias (Elijah) (PBUH)

God sent Elias (PBUH) after the events had been very grievous among Banu Israel; they forgot what God sent to them and they built idols and worshipped them.

It is said that: He is Elias ibn Yasin ibn Fanhas ibn Al'aizar ibn Aaron ibn Amram.

It is said that God was sending prophets to Banu Israel to reminder them with Torah; God sent 1000 prophets from Banu Israel during the time between Moses and Jesus.

Banu Israel took an idol to worship called Baal. God sent them Elias (PBUH) inviting them to worship God exalted is He and they did not obey him. God inspired him that the command of their provision was entitled to him. He supplicated not be rained for three years till their cattle, trees and wild animals all were destroyed. Once, he feared them because he supplicated against them. God inspired to him that there were many creatures were destroyed like animals and birds.

He went to Banu Israel and said "you were destroyed by your sins and you were astray". He asked them to get their idols that they worshiped and ask them to reveal affliction that they suffered. They got their idols and asked them but nothing happened, then they discovered that they were astray. They asked Elias to supplicate for them, he did. God sent them rain that saved them from affliction but they did not repent; they became worse than before. When Elias saw their disbelief, he asked God to hold his soul, so that he could abandon them

Tale of those who succeeded Elias (PBUH)

It is said that Elisha was sent after Elias.

It is said that after Elias was Jonah. Also, it is said that Jonah came after Solomon and Job came after Solomon, too.

Elisha is the son of 'Audai ibn Shuwaylikh ibn Ephraim ibn Joseph. He was an orphan and disabled but Elias supplicated for him to be well and God bestowed him wisdom and prophecy; he was sent to Banu Israel who stayed with them inviting them to monotheism and adhere to path of Elias for a long time till he died.

Tale of those who succeeded Elisha

It is said that there was a young person called Simeon, one of the righteous Israelis. After the death of Elisha, he appointed a man a 60- year old man, called 'Ailoq. He ruled Banu Israel for 40 years. It is said that God was angry with 'Ailoq because of his son who committed adultery and the other son was killed while he was in an army, the Chest was taken by their enemy, then prophecy and rule turned to Shamuel.

It is said: When Elisha died, the sins of Banu Israel were very wicked. By the Chest, which was a remnant of what the family of Moses and the family of Aaron had left, they defeated any enemy stood against them, by God mercy. There was a king, called Eilaph, who ruled them, then there was an enemy who managed to take the chest from them; the king died because of that. The enemy ruled them and they lived in their astray till they repented and God sent them Shamuel. There was in that time a king called Saul who was sent by God. They said, "How can he have kingship over us while we are more worthy of kingship than him and he has not been given any measure of wealth?" Indeed, God chose him over them and increased him abundantly in knowledge and stature. And God gives His sovereignty to whom He wills. Their prophet said to them, "Indeed, a sign of his kingship is that the chest will come to you in which is assurance from your Lord and a remnant of what the family of Moses and the family of Aaron had left, carried by the angels.

They were ruled after the death of Elisha by the mentioned prophets, judges, politicians and enemies oppressing them till God made kingship and prophecy by Shamuel; this period was 460 years. During this period, the first king was a man from the children of Lot called Kosan, he ruled aggressively for 8 years, then, they were ruled by 'Athanil ibn Jephunneh for 40 years. There were many kings who ruled them. Gaalon ruled for 18 years. Then Aylon, a descendant of Ephraim ruled for 55 years. A man called Ahwaz ibn Hanu Alashal, from Benjamin's tribe ruled for 80 years. After then, a king called Yavin from Canaan. Then many rulers came afterward till they asked God to send them a king to defeat their enemies, God sent them Saul.

Tale of Dhul-Kifl

There were many opinions regarding Dhul-Kifl. Some said he was a righteous man and some said he was a prophet. Ibn Abbas said that Dhul-Kifl was Joshua ibn Nun; he was one of Job's children whom God sent him as a messenger for the Levant.

Some scholars said that there was a tyrant from Amalek whom Dhul-Kifl invited to believe in God and he would guarantee the Heaven for him.

The king believed him and became one of the believers till he died. Dhul-Kifl wrote a book by this guarantee and it was buried with him. Dhul-Kifl lived his life in the Levant and he died on 75 year old.

Tale of Jonah (PBUH)

Jonah was after Solomon and some scholars said that Job was between them.

He is Jonah ibn Amittai, he was one of the children of Benjamin ibn Jacob. Before being a prophet, he was a worshipper of Banu Israel who fled to the bank of Tigris where God sent him as a prophet to the people of Nineveh in Mosul when he was 40 years old. It is said that they were people of tyrannical strength. He was uneasy with the message, God inspired him to deliver the message to the their king, accentuating that if they did not respond positively, they would be tortured. A period of 40 days was given to them

God sent them a black fumes-emitting cloud, so they realized that they were about to be tortured, they fled from the village. They asked God to forgive them and accept their repentance. So He did.

When God stopped torturing them, Jonah went out of angry and boarded a ship that shook to the left and the right till he said there was a sinful servant on the ship; they draw lots regarding the one who is going to throw himself in water, they draw lots three times that Jonah is from the losers and he has to throw himself in water. Jonah jumped in the water and then the fish swallowed him. And had he not been of those who exalt God, he would have remained inside its belly until the Day they are resurrected. But God threw him onto the open shore while he was ill and God caused to grow over him a gourd vine.

When the fish gobbled Jonah, he thought in what he had done, he called out within the darkness, "There is no deity except You; exalted are You. Indeed, I have been of the wrongdoers"." "لَا إِلَٰهَ إِلَّا أَنتَ سُبْحَانَكَ إِنِّي كُنتُ مِنَ الظَّالِمِينَ" (21:87).

Some said that he stayed in the belly of the fish for 40 days; some said 7 days and others said 3 days.

Tale of Isaiah ibn Amasiah and the destruction of Jerusalem

He came after Jonah and before Zechariah and he is the one who said tiding of Jesus and Mohammed (PBUT).

God sent Banu Israel prophets together with kings ruling them to be their guidance and He sent nothing for them except Torah that they are always asked to follow.

God sent with the king who ruled them a prophet, Isaiah. That king ruled Banu Israel and Jerusalem for a long time. When that king was ill, the events were grievous, God sent Sennacherib; King of Babylon, along with 600000 soldiers to occupy Jerusalem. God inspired Isaiah to say to the king of Banu Israel to leave the rule and appoint one of his children.

When Isaiah told the king that, he supplicated to God to increase his age. God inspired Isaiah to tell the king that God increased his life for 15 more years and God would save him from his enemy. In the morning, the king found that his enemy was destroyed except Sennacherib and five of his men. God inspired Isaiah to tell the king to let Sennacherib and his men return to their people to tell them about what happened. Sennacherib returned to his people and told them about what God did for his army, then, he died after 7 years.

Some scholars said that this king with Isaiah was Hezekiah whose rule lasted for 29 years till he died. Then, his son assumed the rule for 55 years till he died. After that, his grandsons assumed the rule.

When the king died, Banu Israel competed against each other to assume the rule till they killed each other while Isaiah was among them. God inspired to Isaiah to deliver speech to them. They tried to kill him but he fled till he entered a tree but Satan told them about his place; they cut and sawed the tree while he was inside.

Tale of Persian Kings

East and Babylon were ruled by Kayqubad then Kaykabous who gave birth to Siyavosh. Kaykabous ordered his son to conquer king of Turk "Pharaciab" who asked the king a conciliation then he married his daughter and gave birth to a child. Pharaciab feared that he would take the rule from him, so he killed him. Kaykabous sent those who conquered the Turk and fetched the wife of his son and his grandson "Kaykhusraw" assumed the rule after his grandfather and wanted to take his revenge, so he caught Pharaciab and killed him. Then, he abstained after he ruled the Persians kingdom for 60 years. Then, Lohrasb assumed the rule whereas Jeremiah was sent during his rule.

Tale of Jeremiah

Jeremiah was a prince but he was ascetic and was refusing to marry for fear that it made him busy from worshipping. His father wed him to a woman but he said to her that he did not want women and asked her not to tell anyone about that but she did, so he divorced her. His father wed him to another woman but it was the same. His father wed him to a third woman but he fled till God sent him as a prophet to Banu Israel during king Nashia's ruling because they committed sins and killed the prophets. When Jeremiah delivered the message of God to them, they disobeyed him and did not believe in what he told them. They seized him and put him in the prison till God sent them Nebuchadnezzar.

Tale of Nebuchadnezzar

When Lohrasb ruled and became a king, he sent Nebuchadnezzar to Damascus who set conciliation with its people. Then, Nebuchadnezzar sent a commander from his men to the king of Banu Israel and set conciliation with them but when he went out to Tiberias, Banu Israel killed their king, the commander of Nebuchadnezzar wrote to him about what happened. Nebuchadnezzar marched to Jerusalem and demolished the religious establishments, destroyed the forts, burnt Torah and took the properties. He found the prophet of God, Jeremiah, (PBUH). Nebuchadnezzar knew about his story and sat him free.

Rest of Banu Israel told Jeremiah to ask God to forgive them but God inspired him that they would not repent; implying that if they were honest, they would stay with him in that village. They went to Egypt and said how we would live in a destroyed village. They went to King of Egypt and asked for his help. Nebuchadnezzar conquered Egypt and killed them together with that king.

Tale of conquer of Nebuchadnezzar to Arabs.

Nebuchadnezzar conquered Arabs during the reign of Ma'ad ibn Adnan. It is said that when Adnan died, Arab lands became havoc till Nebuchadnezzar died. Ma'ad together with the prophets of Banu Israel went to Mecca and fought against

Jurhum. Then, he married and got birth to Nizar who gave birth to Mudar, Rabi'ah, Ayad and Anmar. It is said that Mudar and Rabi'ah were Muslims.

Banu Israel were divided; some of them stayed at Hejaz in Yathrib (Medina), others in the Valley of Alqurah.

Then God revealed to Jeremiah to go to Jerusalem and he did but he said to himself "When will be this village rebuild?" Exalted is He says: "He said, "How will God bring this to life after its death?"." "قَالَ أَنَّىٰ يُحْيِى هَٰذِهِ اللَّهُ بَعْدَ مَوْتِهَا" (2:259). So God caused him to die for a hundred years; then He revived him. He said, "How long have you remained?" The man said, "I have remained a day or part of a day." He said, "Rather, you have remained one hundred years." God sent an angel to the king of Persians to go to Jerusalem and build it and live there. It is said he was Uzair. When he went Jerusalem and said to them that he was Uzair and God sent him to them to renew Torah and read it for them. Scholars said that Banu Israel were many after Jerusalem was rebuilt till they were defeated by Romans.

Tale of Zoroaster

It was claimed that he was the prophet of the Magians. He claimed that he was a prophet from God. He came from Balagh, he is Zoroastrian He claimed that the revelation descended on him on Ceylan mountain. His doctrine was still followed till the time of Khosrow Anushiruwan, who prevent following that doctrine. They were not people of a Book; the Prophet (PBUH) took Jizyah from them.

Tale of Yemen Kings

The rule of Yemen after Queen of Sheba was for Yasser ibn Amr ibn Ya'fur. He directed to the Maghrib countries, to conquer them. He reached Valley of sand (locates in Tunisia nowadays). It was hard to cross, that Yasser sent some to cross it yet they did not return.

Tale of Tuba'a

Then, there was the rule of Tuba'a Ibn Zayd ibn Amr ibn Tuba'a ibn Abraha ibn Almanar ibn Alra'ish ibn Qais ibn Saifi ibn Sheba. He marched to Mosul and Azerbaijan where he met the Turks and defeated them. He went back to Yemen, then, he conquered China.

It is said that Tuba'a was Muslim but his people was not. Some said that He was after the time of Jesus.

Tale of Ardashir and his daughter Khamani

Scholars said that Bashtseb faced many wars against Turk and others till he died; his rule was for 112 years and some said 150 years.

His grandson Bohmon ibn Esphandiar ibn Bashtaseb; who was called Ardashir, who ruled all kingdoms around him. The mother of Bohmon was from the children of Saul and his wife was from children of Solomon son of David.

Tale of Daniel

On the reconstruction of Jerusalem, Jeremiah asked God to cause him death. Daniel was from the captives of Nebuchadnezzar when he destroyed Jerusalem, he threw him chained in a well.

God revealed to one from the prophets of Banu Israel to go and get Daniel out of the well.

It is said that Nebuchadnezzar prepared an idol to be worshipped and ordered Daniel and companions to prostrate for it but they refused, so he commanded them to be thrown in the fire but they were not burnt.

Banu Israel returned to Jerusalem and they were living in a good manner till Daniel died, then, the events were bad and there was more injustice till God empowered Artasus who killed and captivated them.

Tale of kings after that

Bohmon died and his rule lasted for 112 years and some said 80 years. Then, his daughter Khamani succeeded, but scholars controverted regarding the reason for her rule. She ruled for 30 years. Her rule was during Kirsh Al'auleimi who ruled Jerusalem and she ruled for 26 years after his death. It is said that the destruction of Jerusalem lasted for 70 years during the rule of Bohmon and his daughter Khamani.

Some said that the destruction of Jerusalem was before that epoch.

Tale of Darius and his children

When Darius ibn Bohmon ibn Esphandiar ibn Bashtaseb assumed the rule, he was given birth to a son who liked him much so he named him after his name. He ruled for 12 years. Then, His son Darius ibn Darius ibn Bohmon Assumed the rule but he was very wicked with his people till he was conquered by Alexander the Great who married his daughter Rushnick bint Darius and conquered India and the east then he wanted to move to Alexandria but he died before reaching it. His rule lasted for 14 years and the rule of Darius was 14 years as well.

Tale of mortality of Darius ibn Darius

When Darius ibn Darius assumed the rule, there was Philip, father of Alexander the Great, who ruled the Greeks and set reconciliation with Darius in return for a yearly land tax. Then, Alexander assumed the rule but he refused to pay the land tax, so Darius was irritated and a great war outbroke between them till Darius was betrayed and killed by some of his guards.

Tales about Alexander

History of Natioans (1)

Some scholars said he was Alexander son of Philip . When the rule of Darius ended, he ruled Iraq, Rome, the Levant and Egypt. He demolished the cities and the forts of the Persians, then, he marched to India and killed its king, after that he ruled China. His tutor was Aristotle and when he ruled, he took him a minister for him and asked for his advice regarding the rule. On either 10 or 11 June 323 BC, Alexander died in the palace of Nebuchadnezzar II, in Babylon, at age 32. There are two different versions of Alexander's death. Plutarch's version is that roughly 14 days before his death, Alexander entertained admiral Nearchus, and spent the night and next day drinking with Medius of Larissa. He suffered a fever, which worsened until he was unable to speak. The common soldiers, were worried about his health, and were granted the right to file past him as he silently waved at them. In the second version, Diodorus recounts that Alexander was struck with pain after downing a large bowl of pure wine in honor of Heracles, shadowed by 11 days of weakness; he did not suffer a fever but died after some agony. Arrian also mentioned this as an alternative, but Plutarch specifically denied this claim.

-
-

The End

The End of Part 1

www.ingramcontent.com/pod-product-compliance
Lightning Source LLC
Chambersburg PA
CBHW022138160426
43197CB00009B/1343